THEOLOGY AND SOCIAL STRUCTURE

Centre for
Faith and Spirituality
Loughborough University

THEOLOGY AND SOCIAL STRUCTURE

ROBIN GILL

MOWBRAYS
LONDON AND OXFORD

ISBN   0 264 66326 8 (paper)
       0 264 66463 9 (cased)

First published in 1977 by A. R. Mowbray & Co. Ltd,
Saint Thomas House, Becket Street, Oxford OX1 1SJ

Printed in Great Britain by
Western Printing Services Ltd., Bristol

Preface

The whole business of trying to give a sociological account of theology represents an obvious academic risk. Even though a number of scholars have hinted that such an account is both possible and potentially important, few have attempted it in any thoroughgoing manner. As yet there are no established guide-lines, mile-stones or border-posts.

Imagine my delight, then, at discovering Gregory Baum's recent book *Religion and Alienation: A Theological Reading of Sociology*. That and the encouraging response of both theologians and sociologists to my own *The Social Context of Theology*, have convinced me that correlations between sociology and theology really do constitute a viable and fruitful area of research. Despite the current monopoly of philosophical and historical approaches to theology, it is possible to envisage the day when a sociological approach to the discipline may prove just as important. Undoubtedly, philosophical and historical methods have made a major contribution to theology within the academic context: but for them, the discipline might never have survived in the contemporary university. Yet I believe that the potential contribution of sociology is as great.

Taken together, this book and the last represent a systematic attempt to convince the theologian that in future he must take full account of the social context, determinants and consequences of his discipline. If my arguments succeed, theological 'truth' may have to be assessed as much in sociological terms as in philosophical or historical ones. The two books also represent a systematic attempt to persuade sociologists of religion to take theology more seriously. Whilst there is no intrinsic reason for the two disciplines to 'dialogue', there are nevertheless mutual benefits to be derived from socio-theological correlations. There is much room here in both sociology and theology for future research.

One of the obvious weaknesses of this book and the last (a dangerous confession to make to reviewers), is that they neglect, ignore, or are just unaware of, a number of sociologists and theologians who have made contributions to this area of scholarship. The sheer *ad hoc* character of these contributions, combined with a dismal lack of seminal studies, makes this a natural pitfall. Even though I have never intended to supply an exhaustive survey of extant literature in this area, I am still aware of this weakness. However, at this stage, the provision of a theoretical framework may be more important than a survey of scholarly opinion.

I am indebted to a number of people who have helped me enormously with the various drafts of this book. Professor David Harned of the Department of Religious Studies at Virginia University has again undertaken the chore of reading a later draft, supplying uncomfortable criticisms and forcing me to work much harder. The Revd W. Graham Monteith also made helpful criticisms of the same draft. Professor David Martin of the London School of Economics again gave me some encouraging early prods. Members of the Sociology of Religion Study Group of the British Sociological Association also provided helpful criticisms of an earlier version of Chapter 2. And my father, Dr Alan Gill, has patiently proof-read both this book and the last—a task only a father would do for a son. In addition, I would like to thank my colleagues at Edinburgh for their encouragement, criticism and stimulation, and in particular Professor James C. Blackie of the Department of Christian Ethics and Practical Theology, who died just before this book was finished.

After all the coffee, sweat and preoccupation I can understand why authors (guiltily) dedicate their books to their wife and family. So finally, my love to Jenny, Martin and Judy.

ROBIN GILL

Contents

Introduction

DESPITE THE early interest of theologians like Ernst Troeltsch, H. R. Niebuhr and the young Dietrich Bonhoeffer[1] in sociology, few theologians have entertained seriously the idea that their own discipline might be subjected to a thoroughgoing sociological analysis. Whilst the last one hundred years has witnessed a quite remarkable openness within Protestant and now Catholic theology to historical and philosophical criticism, there has been no comparable socio-theological criticism. Theologians have generally remained unaware of the ways in which society determines their discipline and the ways, in turn, in which their discipline determines society. The social structure of theology, or rather the interactions that may occur between theology and society, have seldom been subjected to rigorous analysis.

The task of providing an account of the social structure of theology is quite different from that of *The Social Context of Theology*. There I was concerned with exploring some of the methodological problems confronting theologians who wish to use sociology as a discipline ancillary to their own. Granted that theology is never written in a vacuum, but always within a certain social context, I attempted to show that there has been a tendency on the part of theologians either to ignore the sociology of religion altogether, even whilst describing contemporary society, or else to use sociological findings selectively to depict their social context. The focus of an account of the social structure of theology, on the other hand, is on theology itself rather than on the task of the theologian. Theology as a distinct and socially significant discipline is now the subject of attention.

Once the cognitive discipline of theology is treated in this way, the sociology of knowledge at once becomes relevant. In an account of its social structure, theology is regarded at the outset as a socially constructed reality. Whatever its non-sociological validity—which is emphatically not discussed here—theology is demonstrably a human product and as such properly subject to the sociology of knowledge—the discipline which attempts to analyse the relation between human ideas and social structures. It is this sub-discipline of sociology, then, which supplies the theoretical core to this book.

Because the sociology of knowledge is so central to the purposes of this study and because theologians themselves have seldom studied it directly, it is necessary to devote the first chapter to it. The confused nature of contemporary under-standings of the discipline, allied to the difficulties inherent in applying it to a largely unexamined area like theology, make any exhaustive summary quite impossible. Nevertheless, it is still important to select some of the more pertinent features from it in order to show how theology may better be studied.

In Chapter 2 I will begin the main task of this book by examining first the social determinants of theology. These may be of more interest to the theologian himself than the socio-logist, unless he has a prior interest in theology. Despite a general interest in the social determinants of religious beliefs and practices, a specific interest in those of theology is more limited—though, in principle, such determinants constitute a thorough-ly feasible area of research. Despite the obvious classical work of Troeltsch and Weber few contemporary scholars have ventured into this area. It remains, though, a field of peculiar relevance to the theologian.

It is precisely at this point, however, that the sociological perspective appears to become most challenging to the theo-logian. Even if it is admitted that the sociologist is not concerned with the validity or invalidity of theological positions, the task of uncovering their social basis continues to be disturbing. Thus, to suggest, as in Chapter 3, that the Churches' responses to abortion owe as much to contemporary, societal pressures as to independent, moral or theological reflection, is in itself disturbing for churchmen. Doubtless it does not actually in-validate particular defences or criticisms, but it does appear to relativise them. In contrast to other disciplines, as Peter Berger observes, sociology 'raises the vertigo of relativity to its most furious pitch, posing a challenge to theological thought with unprecedented sharpness'.[2]

Despite these obvious dangers of theological relativism, the task of carefully uncovering the social determinants of theology remains an important one. Far from being an attempt to reduce theology to a series of affirmations about society—the charge that is often levelled at Feuerbach—or to relativise it by exposing its obvious dependence upon transitory social contexts, this task of uncovering social determinants becomes an essential step in theological self-awareness. Just as it is widely acknowledged that theological statements carry numerous philosophical and historical connotations and presuppositions, so theologians might eventually assume that an awareness of social context and determinants is a prerequisite of an adequate theology.

This task of analysing the social determinants of theology might also be of interest to the sociologist in general, if only as a way of studying the relation between academic ideas and society at large. In principle, the sociologist of knowledge could study any system of ideology, though, of course, in practice he may be less inclined to study the seemingly esoteric and technical world of theology. In part this may depend on the sociologist's own beliefs and values or even simply on fashion. Nevertheless, in principle, this area of research is open to inspection by the religiously committed and uncommitted alike.

An analysis of the social determinants of theology, however, without a parallel analysis of its possible social significance, would represent a thoroughly imbalanced enterprise. So, I shall argue in Chapter 4, that a serious study of the social structure of theology cannot assume in advance that the theological venture is always epiphenomenal. This is especially true if it is recognised that there are occasions when a theological debate receives a somewhat larger audience than is usually the case. In this context the *Honest to God* debate, the subject of Chapter 5, assumes a level of peculiar importance. For a number of reasons this debate did indeed involve a fairly large number of people who would not normally have engaged in overtly theological discussion. Whatever its theological merits—which are obviously not discussed in this book—the debate is of particular interest to the sociologist. Here the latter is presented with the very real possibility that theology may at times actually determine, as well as be determined by, society.

Given the fact that most contemporary sociologists of religion have largely ignored theology, this thesis might appear somewhat novel. Few have taken seriously the possibility that a socially determined theology might itself prove socially significant: that theology may act as both a dependent and an independent variable within society. Set within the context of Weber, though, its novelty is considerably diminished. Here, at least, was a sociologist who was concerned to analyse the way in which specifically theological ideas may interact with society at large. If for no other reason this thesis does require serious sociological attention.

A study of the social significance of theology may also prove to be important for theologians. Superficially, the logic of *The Social Context of Theology* may have suggested that theology must always be wholly dependent on its particular social situation and can never sit in judgement on current societal assumptions, no matter how fallacious they might be. Such an invidious role for theology would clearly be undermined if it could be shown empirically that theological ideas may sometimes prove influential (though not always in the ways intended by theologians themselves). Clearly no serious sociological analysis could assume such a position on these theological grounds, but it could at least investigate its possibility, even whilst knowing in advance its particular theological consequences.

I will argue at length that any systematic analysis of the social structure of theology must be based upon an interactionist perspective. Thus, it must examine both the social determinants of theology and the possibility that theology may have independent social significance. The interactionist account of theology that I will present in the final chapter is certainly complex. However, anything less complex will inevitably distort an analysis of this actual relationship. Only the unlikely twin possibilities of a society entirely dominated by a single theological outlook or a system of theology entirely divorced from cultural roots would require a less complex form of analysis.

The penultimate chapter represents a digression from the main purpose of this book, since it is concerned, less with the social structure of theology, than with variables actually within theology. Its overall aim will be to show how sociology may be used within 'applied' theology, although at several points it will use the forms of analysis already developed within the book. More specifically, it will maintain that 'prescriptive' understandings of Christian ethics or practical theology tend to allow only for an ancillary use of sociology: whereas 'descriptive/critical' understandings allow for a more integral use of the discipline. In a number of attempts to analyse the relation between faith and action ('descriptive' practical theology) and between faith and moral action ('descriptive' Christian ethics), sociology assumes a crucial role.

In all, four distinct ways in which sociology can be used within applied theology will be isolated. These range from the most ancillary use to the most integral. The most radical of these suggests that theology should take greater account than hitherto of its social consequences—a contention based on a mixture of theological and sociological criteria. The most complex suggests that an analysis of shared patterns of interactions between theological, ethical and social variables, does much to dispel the pluralism evident within Christian ethics. Of course, sociological analysis will not dispel the pluralism to be found amongst contemporary Christians either in their statements on specific ethical issues or in their proposed normative bases for the discipline. Yet, it does suggest that a uniting factor within Christian ethics might well be shared patterns of interaction, rather than specific contents or norms.

A recurrent illustration throughout the book will involve Christian responses to war. This theme offers the sociologist a rich and largely unanalysed source of data and has accordingly been chosen for this reason. It is hoped, though, that it will also provide some continuity to this account of the social structure of theology and show a progression of thought between Chapters 2, 4 and 6. One of the advantages of working in such uncharted territory is that it allows the researcher to explore the more interesting avenues. Nevertheless, it should become apparent, that the following analysis in terms of the sociology of knowledge, could be applied beneficially to many areas of theology. If this book and the last serve to stimulate such research, they will have achieved their purpose.

1

Theology and the Sociology of Knowledge

THIS BOOK will attempt to analyse theology as a social phenomenon, as a 'socially constructed reality'. Whether focusing
upon it as externally determined or determining or internally
varied, theology will always be viewed in purely social terms.
More specifically, it will always be studied from the perspective
of the sociology of knowledge: it is this sub-discipline of sociology which will supply a theoretical core.

There have, in fact, been a number of suggestions recently
that theology as a whole[1] or particular aspects of theology[2]
should be subjected to the scrutiny of the sociologist of knowledge, and not simply to that of the professional theologian.
Strangely, though, these suggestions have seldom taken into
consideration the *ad hoc* accounts of theology that have already
been provided by exponents of this sub-discipline. In this
situation it is essential that an analysis of the social structure
of theology should start with a brief account of some of the
main themes that have been expounded.

To those acquainted with the sociology of knowledge, though,
it will be evident that there is little agreement amongst its
exponents. Fundamental differences abound, particularly between Marxists and non-Marxists, but also between pheno-
menologists and empiricists and between German, French and
American approaches to the discipline.[3] There is no generally
agreed methodological basis, nor even agreement on its application or scope. Some would distinguish sharply between the
sociology of ideology and the sociology of knowledge, whereas
others would reject this distinction as spurious. Some have
argued that it is intellectual ideas which form the primary
material of the discipline, whereas others have claimed that it
is knowledge in everyday life which constitutes this material.

1

The differences between sociologists of knowledge would appear as great, if not greater, than those between sociologists in any other branch of the discipline. Certainly, they would appear to be greater than the differences between those currently engaged in the sociology of religion—a sub-discipline not renowned for unanimity.

Within this situation it is imperative that I should make explicit the particular orientation within the sociology of knowledge that I intend to adopt. It is obviously impossible to offer a history of the discipline, or even an outline of all the different approaches within it, in the course of a single chapter. Nevertheless, it is possible to highlight some of the major themes as they have been related specifically to theology in the *ad hoc* studies of the past. I propose to do this in terms of a progression of four related theses. The first considers theology as 'mere ideology': of all the theses, this is the least refined, but it is the seminal insight from which the others develop. The second considers theology as general ideology: according to this thesis one's own views are subjected to analysis as well as those of one's opponents and theology is placed within the context of all *Weltanschauungen*. The third opposes theology to ideology and represents, as I shall argue, a regression in our understanding of theology. The fourth sees theology as 'socially constructed reality' and suggests the possibility of a thoroughgoing interactionist approach to the discipline, viewing theology alternately as a dependent and an independent variable within society.

A Definition of Theology:

An important prerequisite of an analysis of theology as a social phenomenon, however, is an adequate definition of theology itself. In the absence of any universally accepted depiction of their task by theologians themselves, it is incumbent on the sociologist to provide his own definition, if only to act as a heuristic device. An explicit definition, however arbitrary it might appear to some, at least has the advantage of delineating the subject matter to be considered.

Accordingly, theology may be defined formally as *the written and critical explication of the 'sequelae' of individual religious*

2

beliefs and of the correlations and interactions between religious beliefs in general. This definition of theology in its strictest sense contains a number of sociologically relevant features.

First, it precludes pre-literate religious traditions or myths from consideration. Although oral traditions play an important part in all the major world religions, it is arguable that they are generally different in kind from written explications of religious beliefs. The fact of literacy in itself transforms religious reflection, since detailed systems become possible, as do detailed correlations between beliefs.

Secondly, in terms of this definition theology is concerned with the critical explication of religious beliefs and not with an examination of their overall truth or falsity. The latter belongs properly to the philosophy of religion. Of course, theologians will inevitably be concerned with the truth or falsity of their beliefs—it could not be otherwise within the critical context provided by contemporary universities—but, in so far as they act as theologians they are committed to the overall truth of the beliefs they seek to explicate. They work 'as if' the religious beliefs they are considering are fundamentally true: otherwise (in terms at least of this strictly sociological definition of theology) they cease to act as theologians.

Thirdly, theology is not simply the expression of religious beliefs. It is primarily an intellectual pursuit involving the critical explication of these beliefs. This understanding of theology is both thoroughly cognitive and intellectualistic. Typically it belongs to the role of the academic and not simply to the general religious believer. Further, this understanding of the discipline intentionally excludes from consideration much devotional literature within religious traditions—however socially significant this literature might be. The fundamental sociological differences between devotional literature and theology is that, whereas the former is designed to evoke religious emotions, experiences or beliefs (as are written liturgical symbols), the latter is concerned solely with the explication of beliefs. Theology, then, whilst it remains theology in its formal sense, plays only a secondary role, unlike devotional literature, in fostering the religious life of its participants.

Fourthly, theology does not have to explicate the whole of a

3

belief-system to be theology, although systematic theology *is* an important aspect of the discipline, at least within Christianity. Instead it may involve either the explication of the 'sequelae' of individual religious beliefs or else the explication of the correlations and interactions between these beliefs. The first of these roles in particular allows a fairly wide range of studies to be considered as properly belonging to theology. So, for example, the disciplines of Christian ethics and practical theology qualify as theological disciplines, in so far, that is, as they are concerned with the explication of the 'sequelae' of religious beliefs. Of course, if they are conceived narrowly as normative rather than explicatory disciplines, simply providing Christians with rules by which to live or ministers 'hints and tips' by which to work, they cannot be classified sociologically in this way. Nevertheless, I will argue throughout this book and particularly in Chapter 6 that an explicatory understanding of 'applied' theology is indeed possible and further, that an analysis of it in terms of the sociology of knowledge may yield some important insights.

Finally, this definition of theology employs the ambiguous term 'religious' and does not limit the discipline to the Judaeo-Christian tradition. Certainly, few sociologists today would wish to make a dichotomy between Christianity and religion, as neo-orthodox theologians have often made. Even Berger, after an initial flirtation with the dichotomy,[4] has long since abandoned it. There seems to be no reputable sociological reason for confining theology to Christianity. Indeed, some important research within the sociology of religion has been conducted by abandoning it.[5] Any religion that has generated written explications of its beliefs can properly claim a theology.

Nevertheless, the term 'religious' remains ambiguous, especially when one considers the widely differing interpretations given to it by those holding a functionalist definition and those with a substantive definition. For the former, it would seem that almost any strongly held ideology can count as 'religious'[6] and consequently, that any written explication of ideological beliefs might qualify as theology. This suggests, perhaps, that most functionalist definitions of religion are too clumsy for sociological research[7] and that, within the sociology of knowledge, in particular, they may create considerable confusion in any attempt to distinguish 'religious' from 'political' forms of ideology. Since, however, the present study is confined to a study of theology within the Christian context this problem is not so acute. It is important to stress, though, that in principle this could be a study of Islamic, Buddhist or Hindu theology, even if in practice it is a study of Christian theology. Whatever special problems Christianity may present, the sociologist as a sociologist cannot decide in advance that it is different in kind from all other religions. All theology, whether Christian or not, is equally susceptible to sociological analysis.

Theology as Mere Ideology:

The seminal insight in accounts of the sociology of knowledge as they apply to theology is the specific correlation between differing types of theology and differing types of social structure. If theology is treated solely as an autonomous discipline, regulating its own canons and methods of procedure and owing nothing to society at large, an account of it in terms of the sociology of knowledge is not possible. Whereas it might be possible to present a philosophical or historical account of it, a specifically sociological one would thereby be excluded. Once, however, the observation is made of correspondences between certain theologies and the societies within which they are developed, a genuinely sociological account becomes a real possibility.

There is already an implicit recognition of this possibility in the writings of Francis Bacon, sometimes seen as the earliest pioneer of a sociological approach to knowledge.[8] Amongst the 'idols' that 'beset the human mind' he believes that certain types of theology and philosophy both have a distorting effect and are supported by certain cultural and political contexts.[9] It is the second belief, not the first, which is the original element in his thought. So, to claim that particular theologies are misleading is a commonplace of religious controversy: but, to claim that they derive from socio-cultural and socio-political causes, is not.

However, it is in Karl Marx and Frederick Engels' *The German Ideology* that the first thoroughgoing attempt was made

5

to correlate certain types of theology with certain types of class structure and material behaviour. For Marx, in particular, this marked a radical break from Hegelianism and the beginning of his major work. Not surprisingly, then, it is Hegelian theology which is the principle object of this book and, in particular, the work of the Young-Hegelian philosophers.

There are three distinct features of the analysis of theology provided in *The German Ideology*. First, the authors argued that theology is to be seen as a form of 'ideology'. Secondly, they believed that ideology in general, and theology in particular, reflects a spurious division between mental and material behaviour. And thirdly, they maintained that this spurious division is itself an expression of the privileged, ruling classes, not representing at all the majority of the population. Although all three features were related by Marx and Engels specifically to Hegelian theology, they might be taken to represent a rather broader Marxist critique of theology in general. Together they suggest the thesis that theology is to be regarded by the sociologist of knowledge as 'mere' ideology.

Amongst specialists in Marxism there is, of course, considerable controversy about the scope and exact meaning of Marx and Engels' term 'ideology' and about whether or not they explained its origins solely in terms of economic structures. It is clear, though, that they did identify theology, along with 'morality, religion and metaphysics' as 'ideology' and that they regarded the latter with considerable disdain.[10] This element in itself, though, like the anti-theological polemic of Bacon, was not the original feature of their work. It was the second and third features which represented their unique contribution. Whilst others had bemoaned Idealist theologies, none had advanced the specific socio-structural correlations made there.

The two authors saw theology, as such, as inextricably connected with certain types of social relationship. Further, they imagined that the exposure of this connection thereby discredited it as a legitimate discipline. Granted that they were not particularly interested in theology and that they already believed it and religion in general to be spurious,[11] they nevertheless saw corroboration of its falsity (at least as practised by the Hegelians) in its concentration upon pure thought detached

6

from material behaviour. Within 'ideology' consciousness and conceptions are determinative: within the thesis advanced by Marx and Engels 'life is not determined by consciousness, but consciousness by life'.[12]

The final indication of the spuriousness of theology, however, is given for them in the correlation between the ruling class and ruling ideas, of which theology is a part. They argued that in every epoch the ideas of the ruling class are the dominant ones within society. Thus, 'the class which has the means of material production at its disposal, has control at the same time over the means of mental production, so that thereby, generally speaking, the ideas of those who lack the means of mental production are subject to it'.[13] So the ruling class tends to determine, not simply material productivity, but mental productivity as well.

They argued further, that the division of labour which they saw 'as one of the chief forces of history', in turn, 'manifests itself also in the ruling class as the division of mental and material labour, so that inside this class one part appears as the thinkers of the class (its active, conceptive ideologists, who make the perfecting of the illusion of the class about itself their chief source of livelihood), while the others' attitude to these ideas and illusions is more passive and receptive'.[14] Within this division between mental and material labour, theologians are clearly engaged in the former rather than the latter. Their task, then, is again exposed as ideological and illusory, reflecting a division within the ruling class, rather than referring to the real world. They are a part of the ruling 'intellectual force', whose ideas are taken seriously by others only because they also happen to be a part of the ruling 'material force'. They are a manifestation, therefore, of one class over and against another and of one group over and against another within that class.

On this basis, even the atheistic philosophy of Feuerbach came under attack. The two authors were totally unimpressed by his attempt to reduce theology to humanist philosophy and even by his use of such terms as 'communism'. For them, 'the "liberation" of "man" is not advanced a single step by reducing philosophy, theology, substance and all that trash to "self-consciousness" and by liberating man from the domination of these phrases, which have never held him in thrall'.[15] Instead, they believed, ' "liberation" is an historical and not a mental act, and it is brought about by historical conditions, the development of industry, commerce, agriculture'.[16] Feuerbach, then, like the theologians, reflected the division between mental and material labour and was accordingly judged to be thoroughly inadequate: mental activity *per se* can neither truly reflect nor change the world.

Even from this brief synopsis of ideas from *The German Ideology*, it is clear that theology is regarded as epiphenomenal, socially determined, elitist, intellectualist and finally spurious. However, the analysis it contains may be based on a philosophical error, notably the generic fallacy. By exposing the origins of theology (even supposing their theory based on a correlation between ideas and material behaviour is correct) they imagined that they had thereby exposed its falsity. I have argued elsewhere,[17] that it is important to maintain, that logically origins and validity are separate, even if they are psychologically linked at times. It is quite possible logically to maintain both, that Hegelian theology is dependent on the middle-class background of its originators and, that it is none the less true. This point is especially important if one adopts a wider understanding of the sociology of knowledge than that employed by Marx and Engels. The latter appeared to analyse only *their opponents'* views as socially determined, whereas most recent sociologists of knowledge would wish to analyse *all* views as so determined. On this second interpretation of the discipline, one might trace the origins of all understandings of the world to particular social classes and types of material behaviour. Accordingly, if origins and validity are confused in this way, a thoroughgoing reductionism would appear inevitable: by exposing the origins of views one would thereby be able at the same time to expose their falsity.

However, this interpretation of *The German Ideology*'s analysis of theology misses two crucial features, the one moral and the other axiomatic. The argument against theology is not simply that it is socially determined, but that it is a product of a privileged class. Together with existing philosophy, morality and law, it expresses and seeks to maintain the position of those who have power and privilege at the expense of those who do not. Consequently it is spurious because it is morally, rather than logically, false. Indeed, if the obvious moral component to the polemic contained in the work is ignored, its argument appears to be without foundation, despite its constant appeals to empirical reality. The axiomatic feature springs from this moral one. Granted that theology springs from a morally indefensible background of privilege, it can also be seen to depend on a dichotomy between mental and material labour, the inadequacy of which is axiomatic to the whole book. To accuse Marx and Engels of confusing origins with validity would, in their terms, be simply to range one set of mental activities against another, of indulging in the very type of philosophy to which they were axiomatically opposed. If ideas are not firmly based on empirical reality and material behaviour, they are false by definition—an axiom as intransigent as that later to be proffered by the Logical Positivists.

If this analysis is correct, *The German Ideology* clearly depends on both moral and axiomatic features, which may or may not be shared by contemporary scholars, but which, in any case, can play no crucial part in the sociological methodology I defended in *The Social Context of Theology*. Further, the work is inevitably restricted, in that its polemic is directed against Hegelianism. I shall argue in the final chapter that other forms of theology do not fit its strictures—particularly since they are no longer necessarily the product of a single social class.

Nevertheless, at least one important feature remains in its analysis of theology. It suggested, perhaps for the first time in any thoroughgoing way, that the discipline is not autonomous or socially independent, but rather that an analysis of the relation between theological concepts and social structures is a possible and legitimate enterprise. It is from this seminal insight that the application of the sociology of knowledge to theology can proceed.

Theology as General Ideology:
It was certainly from this seminal insight that the notion of theology as a feature of 'general ideology'—a term associated primarily with the work of Karl Mannheim—could develop.

9

Like Marx and Engels, Mannheim traced the way in which ideas, concepts and consciousness itself are all determined by social structures. Like their work too, his own had an inherent polemical and moral basis: neither was simply disinterested scholarship. Nevertheless, his was considerably more self-critical than theirs and was concerned with methodological problems facing the application of sociological methods to human constructs. Further, he was usually careful to delineate his studies and to make it clear when he was analysing purely sociological claims and when, for example, epistemological ones. Again, unlike Marx and Engels, he did not appear to treat theology (on the few occasions that he used it illustratively) as self-evidently spurious.

Mannheim distinguished between three types of ideology—the 'particular', the 'total' and the 'general' understandings of it—believing that it was only the last which constituted a genuine sociology of knowledge. Under the 'particular' understanding the analyst is sceptical only of 'specific assertions which may be regarded as concealments, falsifications, or lies',[18] whether conscious, semi-conscious or even unconscious. Under the 'total' understanding the analyst is sceptical of the other's total mental structure, that is of 'the opponent's total *Weltanschauung* (including his conceptual apparatus) and attempts to understand these concepts as an outgrowth of the collective life of which he partakes'.[19] However, such analysis does not become sociology of knowledge 'as long as one does not call his own position into question but regards it as absolute, while interpreting his opponents' ideas as a mere function of the social positions they occupy'.[20] For Mannheim, then, Marxism could not qualify as sociology of knowledge, since it evidently had a 'total' understanding of ideology. Under the 'general' form of the total conception of ideology the analyst must have 'the courage to subject not just the adversary's point of view but all points of view, including his own, to the ideological analysis'.[21]

In terms of this 'general' understanding of ideology it can be seen at once that theology would qualify as the proper subject-matter of the sociology of knowledge and further, that the application of the latter to it would not thereby imply any necessary belief in its spuriousness. Theology would be studied, not as the product of 'false consciousness' or of an illegitimate division between mental and material production, but simply, like all other ideas, as a human product. From the perspective offered by the sociology of knowledge, theology would appear, to defenders and critics alike, as a socially constructed reality.

Mannheim's radical understanding of the sociology of knowledge differed, not just from the Marxists' tendency to focus on the views of opponents, but also from Max Scheler's attempt to distinguish between the 'form' and 'content' of ideas. Thus, the latter argued, from a position mid-way between Marxists and Idealists, but owing something perhaps to his Roman Catholicism,[22] that the sociology of knowledge is primarily concerned with the 'form' as distinct from the 'content' of ideas. For Scheler 'the sociological character of all knowledge, of all the forms of thinking, perception, cognition, is indubitable: not, of course, the content of all knowledge and still less its objective validity, but the selection of its objects according to the ruling social-interest perspective . . . the "forms" of the mental acts by which knowledge is won are always and necessarily sociologically co-conditioned i.e., by the structure of society'.[23] In contrast, Mannheim wished to apply the discipline in a thoroughgoing way to both 'form' and 'content', even at the risk of the sort of relativism that Scheler feared. For Mannheim, then, 'the conditions of existence affect not merely the historical genesis of ideas, but constitute an essential part of the products of thought and make themselves felt in their content and form'.[24]

Clearly this radical position raises again the question of the validity of particular ideas. All ideas, with the exception of some of the purely formal and abstract ideas to be found in mathematics, geometry and economics,[25] are now seen as properly subject to the socio-structural analysis of the sociologist of knowledge. In a very real sense they are all exposed as 'relative' to particular social contexts and structures. Indeed, it was one of the desires of both Scheler and Mannheim that all ideas *should* be exposed as relative. Whereas Marx and Engels sought to show that their opponents' views were relative, Scheler sought to relativise scientific positivists[26] and Mannheim political ideologists and utopians in general. All three positions,

11

therefore, were inherently polemical. The last two, however, differed from the first in claiming that no ideas, not even their own, should be treated in absolute terms. It is precisely this position which raises the problems of validity and relativity.

Mannheim was accordingly forced to reconsider the complex relationship between the origins and validity of ideas. He rejected the first view—that of some Marxists—that the exposure of the social determinants of particular ideas necessarily entails their invalidity. He also rejected the second view — that of traditional philosophy—according to which the questions of origins and validity are quite separate. Instead, he offered a further possibility:

> There is a third possible way of judging the value of the assertions that the sociologist of knowledge makes, which represents our own point of view. It differs from the first view in that it shows that the mere factual demonstration and identification of the social position of the assertor as yet tells us nothing about the truth-value of his assertion. It implies only the suspicion that this assertion might represent merely a partial view. As over against the second alternative, it maintains that it would be incorrect to regard the sociology of knowledge as giving no more than a description of the actual conditions under which an assertion arises (factual-genesis). Every complete and thorough sociological analysis of knowledge delimits, in content as well as structure, the view to be analysed. In other words, it attempts not merely to establish the existence of the relationship, but at the same time to particularise its scope and the extent of its validity.[27]

The effect, then, though not necessarily the strictly logical result, of applying the sociology of knowledge to ideas is that they subsequently appear partial and particular. It is difficult for those who hold ideas that have been subjected to such analysis to continue to maintain them as absolutes: they are relativised and particularised.

Of all the elements within Mannheim's account of the sociology of knowledge, it is this which has been subjected to the heaviest criticism.[28] Some would, of course, still maintain the utter separateness of origins and validity, whereas others would argue that, even if there is a link of some sort between the two (a psychological rather than logical one, as I have suggested), it provides the central orientation in Mannheim's work, giving it its inherently polemical basis, instead of being simply a by-product of an otherwise academic discipline. Further, his particular solution to the problem of the apparent relativism created by the sociology of knowledge has attracted criticism. He distinguishes between 'relativism' and 'relationism', believing that the latter is merely the recognition that all historical knowledge 'can only be formulated with reference to the position of the observer'[29] and, as such, is to be preferred to the former as a depiction of the consequences of socio-structural analysis. This distinction is not one which has gained much support: nor has his confidence that the intelligentsia can eventually overcome relativism themselves. Nevertheless, an important part of his argument remains, even if some of his conclusions are not accepted; an effect, albeit a side-effect, of the application of the sociology of knowledge to ideas may be to undermine a dogmatic confidence in them. This remains a strong possibility, even if it cannot be advanced as the *raison d'être* of the discipline.

This possibility is clearly relevant to an analysis of theology in terms of the sociology of knowledge. An attempt to use the latter simply as a means of battering theological opponents, or of discrediting theological dogmatisms in general, must remain suspect unless one is to subscribe to a polemical understanding of the discipline.[30] Yet one of the effects of its application to particular areas of theology may be to raise the 'suspicion' that they are 'partial' and 'particular'. This is a discrete claim, but none the less an important one.

Whatever his polemical motives it is clear that Mannheim intended the discipline of the sociology of knowledge to be a thoroughly rigorous one. He rejected the view of sociology according to which only purely quantitative correlations, largely derivable from statistical evidence, can be counted as properly rigorous. This emerges plainly from the following passage, in which he made one of his occasional uses of a theological example:

When one has stated concerning the ethics of the earliest Christian communities, that it was primarily intelligible in

13

terms of the resentment of oppressed strata, and when others have added that this ethical outlook was entirely unpolitical because it corresponded to the mentality of that stratum which had as yet no real aspirations to rule ('Render unto Caesar the things that are Caesar's'), and when it has been said further that this ethic is not a tribal ethic but a world ethic, since it arose from the soil of the already disintegrated tribal structure of the Roman Empire, it is clear that these interconnections between social situations on the one hand and psychic-ethical modes of behaviour on the other are not, it is true, measurable but can none the less be much more intensively penetrated in their essential character than if coefficients of correlation were established between the various factors. The interconnections are evident because we have used an understanding approach to those primary interdependences of experience from which these norms arose.[31]

Mannheim's interpretation of sociology evidently owed much to Weber's 'humanistic' approach to the discipline. He believed that *verstehen* (the 'attempt to interpret action by understanding the motives of the actor from a "subjective" point of view, i.e., the investigator attempting to put himself in the actor's place'[32]) was a more powerful tool in an analysis of early Christian ethics than statistical correlations.

However, his work has been criticised precisely at this point. So, for example, Robert K. Merton argues that he did not adequately clarify the 'connectiveness' of thought and society. For him, 'once a thought structure has been analysed, there arises the problem of imputing it to definite groups . . . this requires not only an empirical investigation of the groups or strata which prevalently think in these terms, but also an interpretation of why these groups, and not others, manifest this type of thought'.[33]

For Mannheim to have been able to meet this criticism, he would have had to demonstrate why the early Christians alone of oppressed minorities in the Roman Empire developed certain ethical positions. In the process, he might indeed have been forced to take more seriously the theological notions of these Christians, which differentiated them from other minorities. Nevertheless, his overall point remains. Quantitative correlations are not always the most appropriate method of research

14

in the sociology of knowledge. Certainly, in the area of historical theology the sociologist has little option. Such correlations may at times be relevant to a study of contemporary theology, as I shall argue in Chapter 5, but even here it is doubtful if they will be able to provide any thoroughgoing socio-structural analysis of the determinants and significance of particular theological positions. Further, Merton himself admits, that not only are there a variety of research methods open to the sociologist of knowledge, but that there are a variety of types of 'connective-ness' that he might establish between thought and society.[34] It is important only that those analysing the social determinants of theology should distinguish direct, causal determinants from rather looser connections between theological concepts and social structures.[35]

For those concerned with the application of the sociology of knowledge to theology, Mannheim provides an important model. Despite some of his essentially polemical and epistemological concerns and despite his confidence in the intelligentsia and in the 'facts' that the discipline, through them, might uncover, his work remains crucial. A rigorous analysis of the relation between theological movements and concepts, on the one hand, and social structure and culture, on the other, becomes possible, without an assumption that thereby theology is necessarily revealed as a spurious enterprise.

Theology versus Ideology:

An apparent progression beyond this position involves the attempt, through the sociology of knowledge, to discredit, not theology, but ideology. This position accepts, neither the Marxian dismissal of both theology and ideology as spurious, nor the Mannheimian concept of theology as general ideology. It attempts, instead, to exempt theology from the strictures that can be applied to certain other ideas.

This thesis is, at least partially, present in the writings of Max Scheler, particularly in his critique of Comtean positivism. For Auguste Comte, theology, metaphysics and science repre-sented three stages in human thought: theology or religion represented the most primitive, metaphysics or philosophy an intermediate, and positive science the most advanced stage of human knowledge. Scheler, by contrast, held that all three were separate, but equally valid, modes of cognition.[36] In fact, in his attempt to produce a typology of *Weltanschauungen* he even concluded that religious knowledge is considerably less 'artificial' and consequently less open to social change than purely technological knowledge.[37]

It is, though, in the writings of Werner Stark that the attempt to exempt theology from the limitations attached to ideology is most clearly made. Stark believes that a distinction must be made between 'ideology' and 'knowledge', between the 'doctrine of ideology' and the 'sociology of knowledge'. For him, 'the former deals with a mode of thinking which is thrown off its proper course, the latter with all modes of thinking, and especially with those which form the intellectual framework of our whole world-view and which exist long before any falsifying interest-begotten tendency can assert itself'.[38] He apparently accepts a position mid-way between that of *The German Ideology* and that of Mannheim. With the first, he believes that 'ideology' as such is 'off its proper course', 'false' and 'interest-begotten': with the second, he believes that the sociology of knowledge should be concerned with all knowledge, including one's own. He can even imagine that, 'if all men could and would come to control their subconscious and rise superior to the insinuations of selfish or sectional interests, the doctrine of ideology would die off, because there could be no more raw material left in the contemporary world for it to study'.[39]

Stark apparently has some prior way of distinguishing 'knowledge' from thinking that is interest-begotten, that is 'ideology', conceived in perjorative terms. Berger and Luckmann maintain that his position is closer to that of Scheler than that of Mannheim and that for him 'the central problem is the sociology of truth, not the sociology of error'.[40] This is evident in the following passage, which concludes a comparison between theologians of 1270 and scientists of 1870:

> It is not the least valuable service which the sociology of knowledge has to render that it can teach all men humility and charity, both of which are not only virtues of the heart, but potentially also virtues of the intellect. It shows up the essential limitations of one's own knowledge and thereby inculcates

16

humility: it shows up the rationality in the apparent irrationality of the next door neighbour's point of view and thereby inculcates charity. In so far as the truth is the truth only in its proper sphere, the sociology of knowledge contains a precious corrective of that most dangerous and objectionable form of error—arising from abuse of the truth.[41]

Despite an initial similarity to Mannheim's position, this passage moves considerably beyond it. Whereas both Stark and Mannheim argue for a polemical understanding of the discipline as a harbinger of intellectual humility, Stark believes in addition that it can distinguish truth from error. There is an ontological basis to his thought (and possibly a theological basis),[42] which brings his position very close to that of Scheler. This is particularly evident when he argues that, eventually the sociologist of knowledge, 'being, in short, unable to escape the realisation that every mental horizon is limited and confined . . . is all the more obliged to make his way to those uplands from whose summit there is more to be seen than a single culture, a single round and habit of life, and from which, perhaps, who knows, a glimpse may be caught of the verities that are more than products of a narrow valley or a passing day'.[43]

From his writings in both the sociology of knowledge and the sociology of religion,[44] it is evident that Stark views theology as 'knowledge' rather than 'ideology' and, thus, as properly subject to the discipline of sociology of knowledge. However, it is theology, as distinct from the individual theologian, which is really relevant to the discipline, since it involves the use of macrosociology rather than microsociology. For him, 'macro-sociology' is concerned with 'the inclusive society and its influence, the social macrocosm as it were', whereas 'microsociology' is concerned with 'the narrower world of scholarship and art, with the domestic world, so to speak, of the man of scholarship and artistic creation'.[45] Thus a study of the social determinants of particular theological movements would involve macrosociology, but a study of those of an individual theologian would not. Further, in his terms, only the first would constitute a proper study in the sociology of knowledge.

It is extremely difficult to establish any adequate basis for Stark's various distinctions. Not only is it empirically difficult

17

always to distinguish between data belonging to macrosociology or microsociology or between that pertaining to 'knowledge' or 'ideology', but there is no obvious reason for confining the sociology of knowledge simply to 'macrosociology' and 'knowledge'. The effect of Stark's analysis is to produce an arbitrarily constricted discipline.

More critically still, in the present context, the attempt of Scheler and Stark to exempt theology from the strictures they attach to other ideas effectively hinders rather than helps a sociological understanding of theology. The term 'ideology' may well be too value-laden and ambiguous for a rigorous understanding of the sociology of knowledge,[46] but a preparedness to set theological concepts and movements alongside all other intellectualistic concepts and movements, without prior assumptions about their validity, is a prerequisite of such an understanding. Viewed in this way, any attempt to discredit ideology, as distinct from theology, through the sociology of knowledge, represents a regression in a sociological account of theology.

Theology as Socially Constructed Reality:
The final position in accounts of theology viewed in terms of the sociology of knowledge, accepts, not only that it is to be set, without prejudice, alongside other intellectualistic movements in an analysis of its social determinants, but that it, like them, might at times be socially significant. Thus, theology is regarded methodologically as socially constructed, but nevertheless as a social reality. The sociologist must consider, both the possibility that society influences theology and the possibility that theology, in turn, influences society—that is, that theology acts at times as both a dependent and an independent variable within society.

The clearest expression of this position is to be found in Max Weber's *The Protestant Ethic and the 'Spirit' of Capitalism*, to which I shall be returning in Chapter 4. For the moment, it is important to note that Weber was the first to explore, in any thoroughgoing manner, the proposition that specifically theological concepts may have social significance. Whereas he was, at times, concerned to trace the social determinants of these concepts—for example, accounting for the rise of monotheism in socio/political terms[47]—he none the less considered them to be potential independent variables within society. Unlike *The German Ideology*, where theology is viewed as the product of economic and class factors, *The Protestant Ethic and the 'Spirit' of Capitalism* advanced the startling thesis that theological concepts may have influenced economic relations.

However, amongst contemporary sociologists, the notion of theology as a socially constructed reality owes as much to Peter Berger and Thomas Luckmann as to anyone else. Explicitly eschewing the various polemical orientations offered by Marx and Engels, Scheler, Stark or even Mannheim, they claim to 'have bracketed any epistemological or methodological questions about the validity of sociological analysis, in the sociology of knowledge itself or in any other area', considering the discipline to be 'part of the empirical discipline of sociology'.[48] They would clearly disagree with sociologists, like Alasdair MacIntyre,[49] who maintain that sociological and philosophical/epistemological questions cannot be so rigidly distinguished. It is, though, quite possible for the sociologist to focus strictly upon sociological questions, even whilst admitting, with Mannheim, that they are not separable at every point from epistemological ones. Indeed the two authors admit the epistemological nuances of their findings: but they wish, neither to make them central to their understanding of the discipline, nor to unpack their particular implications.[50]

In seeking to redefine the nature and scope of the sociology of knowledge, they bring together a number of elements from Marx, Durkheim, Weber and the psychologist G. H. Mead, in order, like Schutz, to concentrate on 'knowledge' in everyday life. Indeed, they maintain that it is the latter, rather than intellectual 'knowledge', which provides the central focus for the discipline. This marks a critical difference between their understanding of the sociology of knowledge and that of Marx and Engels, Mannheim and Stark, as the following passage demonstrates:

> The sociology of knowledge must concern itself with everything that passes for 'knowledge' in society. As soon as one states this, one realises that the focus on intellectual history is ill-chosen, or rather, is ill-chosen if it becomes the central focus of

19

the sociology of knowledge. Theoretical thought, 'ideas', *Weltanschauungen* are not *that* important in society. Although every society contains these phenomena, they are only part of the sum of what passes for 'knowledge'. Only a very limited group of people in any society engages in theorising, in the business of 'ideas', and the construction of *Weltanschauungen*. . . . To exaggerate the importance of theoretical thought in society and history is a natural failing of theorisers.[51]

Whilst he finds this expressed aim laudable, Peter Hamilton argues that their 'almost wholly gratuitous integration' of fundamentally different theories precludes them from achieving it in any scientific manner. For him 'the integration of disparate sociological positions appears only to be possible at a pre-sociological level . . . virtually all of the empirical insights of Weber, Marx and Durkheim, and to a lesser extent Mead, are submerged in a large speculative excursion into the superficially assimilable elements of their work'.[52]

Berger and Luckmann, of course, would argue that their work is to be seen not as an attempt to integrate disparate sociological positions or to produce 'synthesis for the sake of synthesis', but rather as a new work with particular historical debts, which might even 'do violence to certain thinkers by integrating their thought into a theoretical formation that some of them might have found quite alien'.[53] The point is a fine, but important, one. Nevertheless, Hamilton's main charge, that their work provides few 'testable explanations', that is, that it is in this sense unempirical and unscientific, remains. I have argued elsewhere that it is precisely this speculative and unempirical element in Berger's secularisation thesis which makes it so difficult to evaluate.[54]

Just as serious, though, in the present context is their stress on everyday knowledge at the expense of 'intellectual' knowledge. If Berger and Luckmann's redefinition of the sociology of knowledge is accepted, then clearly an examination of theology will appear as a very marginal activity in its light. This is particularly the case if theology is seen in my terms as the written explication of the 'sequelae' of individual religious beliefs and of the correlations and interactions between religious beliefs in general: this is, after all, an overtly intellectualistic understanding of theology. Marx and Engels and Berger and Luckmann would seem superficially to have something in common—theology and philosophy are regarded axiomatically as epiphenomenal activities. Even though it is evident that the latter, unlike the former, do not thereby consider them to be invalid, they nevertheless do not allow for them to be socially significant.

It is possible that Mannheim and Stark concentrated so heavily upon intellectual knowledge for polemical reasons: they saw within sociology a means of counteracting dominant ideologies with which they disagreed. It is possible, too, that Berger and Luckmann avoided intellectual knowledge just because they in turn wished to escape this polemical bias. Nevertheless, an adequate understanding of the discipline need be committed to neither of these positions. In theory, it is conceivable that intellectual knowledge could form the focus of a particular study without the latter being based either on polemical bias or on over-estimated intellectualism. And in practice, as I shall argue in Chapters 4 and 5, theology may at times be socially significant and, on that account, sociologically interesting.

Despite his stress upon the importance of everyday knowledge, Berger himself does, of course, have an interest in theology. In an important appendix to *The Social Reality of Religion* he even outlines the possibility of a study of the social determinants of theology. Thus, he claims that sociology 'raises questions for the theologian to the extent that the latter's positions hinge on certain socio-historical presuppositions'.[55] Yet at no point in the appendix does he suggest that the discipline might also be socially significant. This second possibility can be deduced only from Berger and Luckmann's more general theory of socially constructed reality. Berger expresses this most clearly elsewhere:

> The relationship between a society and its world is a dialectic one because . . . it cannot be adequately understood in terms of a one-sided causation. The world, though socially constructed, is not a mere passive reflection of the social structures within which it arose. . . . Men concoct theories, even theories that may start out as nothing but blatant explications of social interests,

21

and then discover that these theories themselves become agencies of social change.[56]

Viewed in these terms, theology, like religion in general,[57] would certainly be regarded as socially determined. Yet, once constructed and, particularly, once 'internalised', it becomes a social 'reality' and potentially a socially significant reality.

An Interactionist Approach to Theology:

In the light of these four related theses, even a brief analysis of the works considered suggests that there are radical divisions of viewpoint within the sociology of knowledge. It is apparently impossible either to integrate these divisions in any meaningful way, or to regard them as all contributing equally to a homogenous sociological perspective. Instead, a considerable amount of selection and re-ordering is imperative if a coherent account of the way I intend to apply the discipline to theology is to be given. It will become apparent, though, that my own position is closest to that of Mannheim, whilst remaining critical even of him at certain points.

One point on which all the authors would agree and which must form the seminal basis of the discipline as applied to theology, is that the latter is correlated with social structures. That theology, then, is socially determined and is dependent upon factors within society at large, which might otherwise be considered external to it, must be axiomatic to a study such as this. Even Stark, despite the possibility that there is a theological polemic inherent in his work, is insistent upon this point. The sociologist of knowledge, in studying theology, like the sociologist in general, proceeds 'as if' there were social determinants of everything within it and 'as if' all was explicable in terms of the social.[58] This methodological axiom would appear to be the *sine qua non* of applying the discipline to theology.

Unlike Marx and Engels, however, I do not believe that this contention thereby invalidates the theological enterprise. The essentially polemical function of *The German Ideology* will not intentionally be replicated here. Rather, with Mannheim and most subsequent sociologists of knowledge, I believe that it is vital to apply the discipline equally to one's own views as to those of others with whom one disagrees. If the term 'ideology'

22

is to be retained and applied to theology it can only be defined with Mannheim as 'general' ideology—and certainly not distinguished from 'knowledge' as Stark suggests.

One of my main points of disagreement with Mannheim is, that I do not believe that the polemical character of the sociology of knowledge, in revealing all forms of ideology (including one's own) as less than absolute, should be given so central a place within the discipline. Whilst it may not be possible to separate sociological from epistemological questions as sharply as Berger and Luckmann would seem to imagine, it must surely be possible to recognise the epistemological side-effects of the sociology of knowledge when applied to theology, without at the same time treating them as its *raison d'être*. A degree of theological humility may indeed result from such study, but it may become too biased if it is allowed to be its primary objective.

In general this book will be concerned with macro- rather than micro-sociology (in Stark's sense of the terms). However, I see no legitimate sociological reason for distinguishing too sharply between the two areas and certainly none for regarding only the first as the central one for the sociology of knowledge. Indeed, in the next chapter I will give some attention to the social determinants affecting two individual theologians, namely Augustine and Raven. In principle this should be able to form as important a study as an examination of theological positions in general. Further, it must be admitted that I am not attempting to provide a complete account of theology from the perspective of the sociology of knowledge. For example, I will not offer an analysis of differing patterns of theological socialisation and education in relation to theology as a whole, or even an explanatory account of the origins of theology as a distinct human activity. A measure of selectivity is inevitable.

In contrast to Berger and Luckmann, I will be concerned with an area of intellectual knowledge and not with everyday knowledge, as important as the latter undoubtedly is. This concentration stems from a conviction, shared with Mannheim and Weber, that the former may at times be socially significant, that is, that the effect of intellectual ideas may not always be confined simply to intellectuals. In relation specifically to theology, this contention necessitates the adoption of an inter-actionist approach. For Marx and Engels and possibly also for Berger and Luckmann, theology is always viewed as a depend-ant variable, as solely determined and never capable of in-dependent determination. From an interactionist perspective, however, the possibility would be allowed that theology may at times act as both a dependent and an independent vari-able.

This point is crucial and subject, perhaps, to misinterpret-ation. I have already suggested that the sociology of knowledge is methodologically committed to the view that theology is socially determined. It certainly cannot, whilst remaining a strictly sociological discipline, entertain the view that only particular features of theology are socially determined and other features are not. That would be, I believe, to commit a socio-logical blunder.[59] Nevertheless, once a particular theological position becomes a social reality (albeit a socially determined reality), the possibility cannot be excluded *a priori* that it may act as an independent variable within society. Indeed, an interactionist approach allows that such a position may be simultaneously determined and determining. Of course, such an approach tells the theologian little about the validity of his ideas, though it may tell him something about their effective-ness. The notion of theology acting at times as an independent variable is not to be confused with the notion of it being an 'autonomous', 'independent' or even 'God-given' activity—though it may be considered to be these things on other, non-sociological grounds.

Finally, I should stress, with Mannheim, that the application of the sociology of knowledge to theology must be thoroughly rigorous. I will be critical at times, particularly in Chapters 2 and 4, of other attempts to analyse the social determinants or significance of theology. It is not only that such attempts have tended in the past to be *ad hoc* rather than systematic, but that they have sometimes been far too speculative and lacking in any sociological rigour. Naturally it would be inappropriate to demand quantitative statistical correlations in studies that are often concerned with historical theology, but it is important that socio-structural analysis should proceed with caution and rigour. In the case of contemporary theology, an adequate analysis of it should be capable of generating testable hypotheses. If sociological rigour has not always been the hallmark of past accounts of theology it could be so of future ones.

2

The Social Determinants of Theology

LIKE MOST other aspects of the sociological investigation of theology a study of its social determinants has been curiously ignored by sociologists of religion and knowledge alike. It will be the aim of this chapter and the next to explore this fruitful area of research—first by critically analysing some of the *ad hoc* studies that do exist, and then, in the second half of this chapter and the following one, by suggesting fresh avenues.

In the light of the concluding remarks of the previous chapter it must be conceded at once that a study of the social determinants of theology represents an imbalanced enterprise, since it treats the discipline solely as a dependent variable within society. The sort of interactionist perspective that I have already defended would require the sociologist of knowledge to take seriously the possibility that theology may act at times as both a dependent and an independent variable, as both determined and in turn determining. Any examination of just one of these possibilities clearly distorts this interactionist perspective.

Certainly some of the pioneer social scientists entertained the idea that religion in general, as distinct from theology in particular, may have these twin functions. In a review of Marx, Freud, Durkheim, Weber, James, Niebuhr and Malinowski, the sociologists Glock and Hammond suggest that in them 'religion was treated as both a dependent and an independent variable . . . variations in the form and content of religion came to be understood as a result of observable natural, rather than unseen and unseeable supernatural forces, but religion also came to be recognised as an independent variable helping to shape personality and helping to create, reinforce, or challenge forms of social organisation'.[1] Of course they varied considerably in the balance they gave to these two functions of religion—Marx and

27

Freud treating religion as more dependent than Weber or James—nevertheless, an interactionist approach is present to some degree in all.[2]

I shall argue in Chapter 4, that of all the pioneer social scientists it was Weber who took most seriously the possibility that religious beliefs and even theological ideas, could be socially significant.[3] Certainly, by comparison, Durkheim[4] tended to treat such beliefs mostly as dependent variables. In *The Elementary Forms of the Religious Life* they play a secondary role to man's need for social cohesiveness and, at the most, they act as conservative agencies, maintaining the *status quo* of particular undifferentiated societies.[5] They could never act, as in Weber, as agencies enabling social change. Even in *Suicide*, despite his observation of significantly differing rates of suicide amongst Catholics, Protestants and Jews, Durkheim attached little importance to religious belief as an independent variable. He specifically rejected the idea that it is differing beliefs in God, after-life or damnation which are responsible for differing rates of suicide. The considerably higher rate amongst Protestants cannot be attributed to these factors, since 'the Protestant believes in God and the immortality of the soul no less than the Catholic'.[6] Thus, 'the beneficent influence of religion is . . . not due to the special nature of religious conceptions': instead, 'if religion protects man against the desire for self-destruction, it is not that it preaches the respect for his own person to him with arguments *sui generis*; but because it is a society'.[7] More specifically, it is the relatively monolithic nature of Roman Catholicism and 'less consistency' of Protestantism that are responsible for their respective rates of suicide. The breakdown of dogma and the lack of common beliefs and practices in the latter are responsible for its lack of social cohesiveness and its consequent proclivity towards suicide. It is apparent, then, that the function ascribed to religious belief in *Suicide* is similar to that in *The Elementary Forms of the Religious Life*: it is socially significant only as a conservative agency and only in so far as it serves to maintain an existing society.

Real differences exist, then, between these two pioneer sociologists, but it is still possible to argue that they and others, to a greater or lesser extent, adopted an interactionist approach to religion. Certainly, the amount of their studies concerned with religious phenomena suggests that they regarded religion itself as a key factor within society—however spurious they might privately have thought it to be. Few of them, though, thought theology worth considering.

As against such interactionist perspectives, a separate treatment of the social determinants of theology must appear thoroughly one-sided. In Chapters 4 and 5, though, it will be balanced by a similar separate study of the social significance of theology. In addition, it is arguable that separate attention of this sort carries certain distinct advantages for both the sociologist and the theologian. If nothing else, it may help them to clarify the particular points of pertinence to their respective disciplines that accrue from these two foci.

The theologian may be reluctant at first to admit the importance of studying the social determinants of his discipline, particularly when he discovers that his ideas are as subject to inspection as those of his opponents. At least two constraints might serve to exacerbate this reluctance. On the one hand, he might fear the theological relativism that appears to result from such study[8] and on the other, he may be suspicious of the social determinism on which it is apparently based.[9] As I have already argued, this fear may be founded on a confusion between the origins and validity of ideas and the suspicion may be grounded on a false identification of methodological social determinism with ontological social determinism. Further, even in the event of this second type of determinism being adopted, he might pursue Berger's theological suggestion that, 'man projects ultimate meanings into reality because that reality is, indeed, ultimately meaningful, and because his own being (the empirical ground of these projections) contains and intends these same ultimate meanings'.[10]

As a feature of man's attempt to build *Weltanschauungen*, theology becomes of direct relevance to sociologists who might otherwise be little interested in its contents. Sociologically, it provides important examples of socially determined intellectual thought. In addition, it may reveal something of the 'inner-layers' of religiosity to the sociologist of religion.[11] An

29

analysis of the social determinants of theology carries both sociological and theological implications.

Social Determinants of Individual Theologians:

The most obvious source of research into the social determinants of individual theologians is their biographies. The sensitive biographer should indicate the social context of his subject and, in the instance of an academic subject, the likely social sources of his ideas. Inevitably, though, biographers vary in their knowledge of sociology. Some, like Peter Brown, the biographer of St Augustine,[12] have gone to considerable lengths to equip themselves with an understanding of the social sciences, while others remain comparatively ignorant of them. Nevertheless, even non-sociologically oriented biographies, like that of the Anglican theologian Charles Raven, to whom I shall return presently, are able to furnish important research data for those interested in the social determinants of theology.[13]

Peter Brown gives an excellent example of the study of the social determinants of an individual theologian when he compares Augustine's response to misfortune with that of Libanius:

> What one must seize, however, are the deep reasons that would lead a man like Libanius, almost an exact contemporary of Augustine, to react to a dream as an omen of '(magical) medicines, spells and attacks on me by sorcerers', while Augustine will say, of the terror of dreams, that they 'show clearly that, from our first root in Adam, the human race stands condemned to punishment'.[14]

Brown rejects traditional explanations which suggest that sorcery was on the increase in the fourth century AD due to the decline of traditional religions and the rise to power of 'semi-Christians' within the Roman state. Given such explanations, it might seem reasonable that Libanius should cling to the ways of the past, whilst Augustine, following his conversion, should be keen to contest them. But two factors, in particular, strike Brown as incongruous. First, he thinks it is far from clear that there was any real rise in either the practice or fear of sorcery during this period. And secondly, such explanations do not account for the fact that Augustine's response to misfortune is so all-encompassing.

In relation to the first factor he argues that 'Late Roman society was dominated by the problem of the conflict between change and stability' and that, as a result, 'we find a situation which has been observed both to foster sorcery accusations and to offer scope for resort to sorcery'.[15] It is not so much that Libanius is clinging to a passing order, but that he is responding to a stable one. Sorcery for him could account for incongruities in an otherwise fixed order. Man's identity is so static that incongruities occurring require a daemonic explanation. This understanding of sorcery, it should be noted, owes much to Evans-Pritchard's concept of sorcery as 'a function of situations of misfortune'.[16]

On the other hand, Brown argues that in his later writings Augustine widened his doctrine of the punishment of the human race for the sin of Adam to cover all misfortune—'misfortune, indeed, has eclipsed voluntary sin as the object of the old man's bleak meditations'.[17] For Augustine, existing in a personally highly unstable social context, man's identity was far from fixed and human discrepancies were the norm. Further, the Christian Community as a whole, during the third and fourth centuries, tended to be recruited from the rootless peasants coming from the country—themselves contributing to the sense of discrepancy felt by Augustine.

Overall, then, it was not simply theological notions that fashioned differences between the responses of Augustine and Libanius to misfortune, or which caused the gradual demise of the latter. Social context was crucial:

> In the fourth and fifth centuries, therefore, the sense of a fixed identity in a stable and well-oriented world, that would encourage the blaming of sorcerers and would single out incongruities in public behaviour as *the* misfortune *par excellence*, was being eroded in both the social milieu and the religious ideas associated with the leaders of Christian opinion.[18]

Whatever its merits in terms of the available historical evidence, Brown's analysis offers the sociologist a highly attractive model for the study of the social determinants of an individual theologian—and in the process makes a significant contribution to the understanding of sorcery as a social phenomenon.

Social Determinants of Theological Positions:

The *ad hoc* studies of the social determinants of theological positions in general may be divided into three main groups; socio-cultural studies, socio-political studies and socio-ecclesiastical studies. They are not, of course, mutually exclusive and sociologists who have considered particular theological positions have often used more than one approach. Nevertheless, they do represent three distinct groups and examples of each may be given from the sociology of religion.

A number of studies of the way theologians reacted to a supposed process of secularisation during the 1960s provide a good example of the first group—i.e. socio-cultural studies of the social determinants of theological positions. I have argued elsewhere[19] that the secularisation model played an important part in much of the theology of the 1960s and that, whether or not an actual process of secularisation really existed, it was thought to exist by those theologians and consequently had a very real influence upon them.

Bryan Wilson has argued that theology during that period was radically affected by secularisation. Most obviously it undermined the confidence of theologians in their task:

> One consequence of the expansion of modern knowledge has been its increased influence on theological studies. Without usually becoming expert in such disciplines, theologians have recognised how vulnerable is their discipline to influences from outside—of which archaeology, comparative religion, anthropology, psychology and sociology are perhaps the most relevant.[20]

Given this lack of confidence, theologians have increasingly looked to ecumenism as a substitute—'in an age when Christianity has been demythologised, when traditional ideas about God have been radically challenged by bishops of the Church, ecumenism becomes a new faith—something to believe in'.[21] Alternatively, theologians turn to some form of exclusive sectarianism.

Wilson, then, believes that the process of secularisation apparent within the West, whereby 'religious thinking, practices and institutions lose social significance',[22] radically alters contemporary theology. This is a view shared and worked out more systematically by Peter Berger. For him, the appearance

32

and dominance of neo-orthodoxy under the inspiration of Karl Barth represented only a temporary interruption (itself having obvious social determinants in two World Wars) in an overall process of secularisation. The true process, as distinguished from the temporary interruption, is represented by the old liberal theology of Schleiermacher and Harnack and the neo-liberalism of John Robinson and Harvey Cox:

> The contemporary eruption of what may well be called 'neo-liberalism' thus takes up where the earlier liberalism left off, and just because of the intervening period does so in considerably more 'radical' ways. The latter fact may then also be ascribed to the more penetrating effects of secularisation become more mature, as well as to the increasingly world-wide and permanent establishment of a pluralistic situation.[23]

Both Wilson and Berger were, until recently at least, proponents of a thoroughgoing secularisation model. However, even those normally critical of the model[24] might accept that many theologians during the 1960s (and possibly still today) were peculiarly influenced by it. It has been, after all, a highly persuasive and recurrent model.

Socio-political studies of the social determinants of theological positions range from Swanson's thoroughgoing attempt to relate theistic beliefs to political structures, to the more *ad hoc* observations of others. They represent, however, an important factor within the sociological study of theology.

G. E. Swanson[25] set out to demonstrate a specific correlation between certain types of theistic belief and certain types of political structure. Weber, of course, had already suggested that 'the growth of a world empire in China, the extension of the power of the Brahmin caste throughout all the varied political formations in India, and the development of the Persian and Roman empires favoured the rise of both universalism and monotheism'.[26] Further, Durkheim had already suggested a direct link between the origin and function of religion and man's sociability. Swanson accordingly advanced the specific thesis that monotheistic belief is always to be found in societies containing three or more hierarchies of sovereign groups.

It is interesting to note that even those who are highly critical of Swanson's overall thesis, allow on occasions that he may have suggested important social determinants. Thus, Bowker, who disagrees with his general thesis, makes an admission to this effect:

> Because the evidence even as it stands is ambiguous and contradictory of the hypothesis, it is extremely likely that the correct interpretation of the evidence is that there are resources of meaning in the construction of human senses of reality in addition to the social as such. This does not in the least invalidate Swanson's correlations between particular conceptualisations and particular social, constitutional realities. What it does suggest is that what Swanson is analysing is not the *origin* of the sense of God, but the ways in which some senses of God, which may well be derived initially from *other* resources of meaning, are expressed or clothed imaginatively.[27]

Bowker's point is important—and possibly more radical than he imagines. As an attempt to uncover the social origins of religious beliefs *The Birth of the Gods* may be no more successful than *The Elementary Forms of the Religious Life*. There are, after all, crucial methodological difficulties facing all those who wish to expose these origins. Yet as a study of the social determinants of theological positions it may indeed have value: it need no longer be confined to pre-literate religious beliefs, but could be extended to cover theology understood as the 'written explication of religious beliefs'.

A second example might be taken from a sociologist who is concerned more with contemporary theology than the origins of religious beliefs. In his examination of the former, Roland Robertson disagrees with Weber's contention that 'the salvation sought by the intellectual is always based on inner need, and hence it is at once more remote from life, more theoretical and more systematic than salvation from external distress, the quest for which is characteristic of non-privileged classes'.[28] The 'Death of God' theology of the 1960s showed the opposite tendency—a thoroughly profane orientation, almost indistinguishable from sociological analyses of 'civic religion'. To explain this situation, Robertson suggests that intellectualism has become a more diffuse phenomenon in the mid-twentieth century. In particular, 'in the institutional-religious sphere theologians have been exposed to increasingly extensive ranges of educational and general, socio-cultural experience . . . they have also been confronted with many very visible groups of internationally-focused non-religious intellectuals'.[29]

Whereas Bryan Wilson tends to explain the so-called 'Death of God' theology as itself a manifestation of the process of secularisation, Robertson appears to favour a more socio-structural explanation, in terms of the greater contact of theologians both with other religions and with irreligion. Naturally, this does not offer a total explanation, since particular theologians may and do respond to religious pluralism with some form of sectarianism. The religious 'enclave' remains a possibility for twentieth-century *homo religiosus*.[30] Nevertheless, it may partly account for the sociologically unusual phenomenon of 'Christian atheism'.

Finally, socio-ecclesiastical studies of the social determinants of theology have tended to emerge from the ever-expanding studies in Church/Sect typology. The 'grand' attempts of Ernst Troeltsch and Werner Stark to analyse ecclesiastical structures and their theological entailments over a span of history, naturally furnish the sociologist with numerous examples of this particular approach. Troeltsch, especially, has provided the seminal basis for contemporary Church/Sect typology— even though few today would follow his analysis closely and even fewer would recognise the fundamentally theological axiom of his work.[31] In his depiction of many of the theological differences between churches and sects, however, his work remains highly informative.

It is, though, Bryan Wilson's work on sects which has most fully documented and analysed some of the features of sectarian theology. His current seven-fold differentiation between one sect and another rejects a specifically theological or doctrinal basis of classification and instead adopts the central criterion of the sect's 'response to the world'.[32] In the process, however, he is better able to expose the social determinants of a particular sect's theology. In addition, his earlier work on the Elim, Christadelphians and Christian Scientists,[33] uncovered some of the processes of religious socialisation, by means of which minority religious groups maintain ideas that are largely implausible within society at large. Undoubtedly, Church/Sect

35

typologies still face major problems arising from the varied criteria used by sociologists to make differentiations. As a result, some sociologists of religion have abandoned them in favour of the study of religious culture, symbols and ideas.[34] Nevertheless, it is still possible that the latter owe as much to ecclesiastical structures as to anything else.

Theological Responses to War:

The *ad hoc* nature of existing studies of the social determinants of theology is evident even from this brief and selective analysis. Whereas others have indeed discussed these determinants in the past, they have seldom done so in any systematic fashion. At the most, they offer hints, not a rigorous or thoroughgoing framework for analysis.

As a result, it is crucial that each stage in the formal analysis of theology in terms of the sociology of knowledge should be justified through a rigorous use of case-studies. I believe that the theme of theological responses to war offers the analyst peculiarly fruitful material. Although, perhaps, not central to many systems of religious belief, reactions to the ethical issue of war none the less involve important *sequelae* of such belief. In so far as they do and in so far as they are written and not oral, they clearly conform to my definition of theology. Furthermore, the theological problems created by the ethical issue of war have received considerable attention from a number of individual theologians, including both Augustine and Raven.

Even the most cursory examination of theological attitudes within Christianity to war and peace reveals a strange discrepancy—a discrepancy which certainly merits the attention of the sociologist. One expert in Church history describes this discrepancy in terms of two historical claims. The first is, that 'the age of persecution down to the time of Constantine was the age of pacifism to the degree that during this period no Christian author to our knowledge approved of Christian participation in battle'.[35] The second is, that 'the accession of Constantine terminated the pacifist period in church history'.[36] Bainton does point out that this contrast can be made too sharp. The pacifism of the early church ranged from the absolutism of Tertullian to the pragmatism of Origen and there were known

36

to be soldiers who were also Christians, at least from the end of the second century. Further, the transition effected by Constantine took some twenty years to complete, during which time Christians increasingly joined his army, fighting under the symbol of the cross. Nevertheless, a clear discrepancy exists which requires explanation; first St Ambrose and then St Augustine articulated a just-war theory for Christians, borrowing heavily from classical rather than New Testament sources, in a way which would have been impossible for earlier theologians.

The situation of the pre-Constantinian Church appears all the more remarkable when it is realised that no major Christian church or denomination has been consistently pacifist since Constantine. Indeed, Christian pacifism has been largely confined to a small group of sects, such as the Quakers, Anabaptists, Mennonites, Brethren and Jehovah's Witnesses. Further, pacifists within churches, as distinct from sects, have in times of war been barely tolerated by their fellow Christians.

The reception by distinguished churchmen of Raven's pacifism during the 1930s is highly instructive in this context. Raven himself had attempted to enlist three times in 1914, being turned down on each occasion on health grounds, and eventually became a chaplain in the Flanders trenches. He only became a thoroughgoing pacifist in 1930 although he remained one for the rest of his life, writing several books defending Christian pacifism.[37] Yet he was still able to write that 'I have seen war without horror and can appreciate and share its appeal to mankind'.[38] Further, he thoroughly disliked the attitudes of some of his fellow pacifists:

> If I may be frank, when I listen to some of my peace-loving friends, their arguments arouse an instinctive antagonism: their horror of death, the falsity of their picture of war, their failure to recognise the existence of human beings whose religion glorifies fighting, their inability to resist the appeal to fear and to disgust, as if Satan could ever cast out Satan—these things merely fill me with a vast admiration for the simple heroism of the lads I buried somewhere in France.[39]

Nevertheless, by 1945 he wrote in a private letter that 'my faith isn't strong enough to survive the regular reading of

Church papers'.[40] In 1935 no less a figure than William Temple had suggested that his position as a pacifist was 'heretical in tendency' and he subsequently exchanged numerous letters debating pacifism in the columns of *The Times*. At one stage he even accused Temple, who was then Archbishop of York, of 'apostasy'.[41] Clearly, as a pacifist within the Church of England, he was regarded and regarded himself as an 'outsider' (unlike many other previous Regius Professors of Theology, he was never offered a bishopric!).

Two factors, in particular, might serve to heighten this sense of discrepancy for the sociologist between the pre-Constantinian and post-Constantinian churches. The first concerns the way in which the apparently pacifist-oriented New Testament evidence has been used and the second the way in which just-war theories themselves have been developed, despite obvious inherent circularities of argument.

Historically speaking, the New Testament has been used as a basis for all of the three main Christian responses to war—pacifism, just-war and crusade.[42] Crusaders tended to use the story of Jesus' cleansing of the temple and the sentence 'I came not to send peace, but a sword'. Just-war theorists have tended to use sentences like 'Render to Caesar the things that are Caesar's' or Romans 13. The pacifists have been able to use the more obvious material, such as that in the Sermon on the Mount, urging Christians to 'resist not evil, turn the other cheek, go the second mile, love your enemies'.

It is significant that, not only is the pacifist-oriented material in the New Testament considerably less ambiguous than that used by just-war theorists,[43] but that the latter almost invariably resort to arguments from silence. The Roman Catholic moral theologian Eberhard Welty provides an interesting example of this. As a just-war theorist he first points out that the Old Testament is undeniably militarist, but his argument changes when he comes to the New Testament:

> Concerning war the New Testament must be considered in its entirety. Statements conditioned by the circumstances of the time cannot be regarded as universally valid and binding. Neither Christ nor the apostles condemned war or military service. Christ was sent into the world by the Father in order

to establish the messianic kingdom of peace. But men rejected him and his Gospel, and thereby forfeited the promises that were directly linked with the coming of Christ. Henceforth they had to take up the cross and suffer with Christ. . . . War is one of these great trials and punishments of this life.[44]

The argument from silence is sometimes developed still further. Not only, it is argued, did Jesus never condemn military service, but he implicitly accepted the *Pax Romana* which depended on the potential and at times actual use of force. Like all arguments from silence, however, it should alert the sociologist to search for social determinants.

The second factor to note concerns the evident circularity of even the most sophisticated just-war theories. Despite the combined brains of Ambrose, Augustine and Aquinas these theories are still comparatively undeveloped. The form in which the theory is put in a celebrated British Council of Churches' publication well illustrates this point:

For a war to be 'just' it must
(i) have been undertaken by a lawful authority;
(ii) have been undertaken for the vindication of an undoubted right that had been certainly infringed;
(iii) be a last resort, all peaceful means of settlement having failed;
(iv) offer the possibility of good to be achieved outweighing the evils that war would involve;
(v) be waged with a reasonable hope of victory for justice;
(vi) be waged with right intention;
(vii) use methods that are legitimate, i.e., in accordance with man's nature as a rational being, with Christian moral principles and international agreements.[45]

The publication admits at once that 'the obvious weakness in this whole conception is that in the absence of any competent authority, every nation is a judge in its own cause. Almost every clause contains words which raise the question "in whose opinion?" Is there any right which someone does not doubt?'[46] Similarly, Welty, having stated that wars of aggression are immoral, admits that 'it is difficult to state exactly which wars should be considered wars of aggression'. His own rather optimistic solution is to rely upon an international tribunal which 'fulfils all the conditions for a really unbiased and objective judgement'.[47]

The more radical point, though, which neither publication admits, is that their accounts of the just-war theory are frankly tautological. Thus, within the account already quoted, the actual term 'justice' is used, in addition to similar terms like 'right', 'good' and 'legitimate'—and all this in an account which purports to specify the preconditions for a 'just-war.' Such circularity would appear to be endemic in just-war theories.

When these two factors—the tenuousness of the New Testament exegesis of just-war theorists and the circularity of their formal arguments—are combined with the empirical observation that 'the massive constraints that religious leaders may impose on any support they are willing to give war tend to fade away in the heat of actual battle',[48] the full incongruity becomes apparent. The fact that both church leaders and theologians before Constantine were not prepared to sanction war, whereas those since Constantine have been so prepared, requires sociological explanation. The specific social determinants might be analysed in terms of the three approaches noted earlier; socio-cultural, socio-political and socio-ecclesiastical.

At the socio-cultural level, it is possible that the newly found majority status of Christianity with the accession of Constantine to power, involved it in greater exposure to cultural pluralism. Previous attempts by the Gnostics and others to expose Christianity to a wider cultural base had generally been labelled 'heretical'. As a minority religion Christianity could afford a good deal of 'cultural purity'. However, as a religion catering for the majority of a given population it was at once faced with a wider culture.

It is no accident, then, that Augustine was able to borrow quite freely from classical sources to build his just-war theory. In previous, minority-status, times a greater adherence to New Testament precepts might have been expected, unless his work was to be dubbed 'heretical'. Given his new audience, drawn from a wider spectrum than the Judaeo-Christian one of the past, classical borrowings became possible and plausible. Indeed, it has been possible for Christians ever since—particularly within Roman Catholic, Anglican and Lutheran traditions—to adopt just-war theories which have little reliance on the New Testament and which differ very little, if at all, from general humanistic attitudes to war. Certainly, the majority of the Church of England's hierarchy, who reacted against the pacifism of Raven, differed very little in their attitudes from those of society at large, Christian or otherwise. During the First World War this correspondence between the views of, say, the Anglican Bishops and generals was even closer: the 'war to end all wars' was encouraged in many sermons.

At the socio-political level, it is possible that Augustine was faced with at least two immediate problems. In the first place, he was confronted with the increasingly successful barbarian invasion of the Roman Empire and with the consequent taunts from the pagans that this situation was a direct product of the Christianisation of the people. In the second place, he could forsee the very real possibility of the collapse of the *Pax Romana*. The latter undoubtedly assisted the spread of the Gospel, since it made effective communication possible. Formerly, it could simply be assumed by Christians and needed little defence or justification: now there was plenty of evidence that without the use of a certain amount of force it would collapse, with seemingly disastrous consequences for Christianity.

Again, once Christianity assumed majority status, it could no longer afford to ignore the fate of political regimes. As a minority religion political factors were comparatively irrelevant to it. It was not so necessary then for Christian organisations to be in harmony with the political sympathies of the majority of the population as it was to be later. Thus, the fate of the Roman Empire might have been a matter of comparative indifference for Christians had not Constantine effectively installed them as representatives of the majority religion. Indeed, within political situations today in which Christians are in a minority, the particular fate of regimes may be a matter of comparative indifference. It is certainly interesting that the institutional churches in Britain had declined fairly rapidly between the whole-hearted acceptance given by them to the First World War and the more cautious acceptance afforded to the Second.

Finally, at the socio-ecclesiastical level some of the findings of contemporary Church/Sect typology are directly relevant. It

41

is tempting for the sociologist to analyse the pre-Constantinian church in sectarian terms and the post-Constantinian church in more specifically church-oriented terms. Certainly the minority status of the former and the majority status of the latter give credibility to such an analysis—though these factors in themselves are not sufficient to justify it fully, since a sect is not simply a minority movement, nor a church a majority one.

Yinger expresses the difference between a church and a sect, in the context of war, very aptly. Having noted that, in a crisis, church spokesmen may shift very swiftly from a general condemnation of war to the specific acceptance of an actual war, he argues:

> The sociological meaning of 'church' as a religious institution thoroughly integrated with a society, as well as the concept of the dilemma of the churches, can help us to interpret this shift. It is inconceivable that a church—by its very definition—should fail to support a nation in a major war. Church leaders could scarcely hope to be effective in a society if they turned away completely from the basic struggle in which that society was engaged. They accept the reality of much that is inevitable, so far as their own power is concerned, in order—it is their hope—to be able to exert a qualified influence.[49]

The sect, on the other hand, has no such necessary role. Yet, of course, the majority of sects (on any definition of the term) have not been pacifist-oriented. Further, as Yinger himself admits, the sects that are pacifist-oriented 'exhibit a wide range in types of opposition to the claims of the state in war'.[50] This is hardly surprising, since, as already indicated, Wilson has shown how varied are particular sects' 'responses to the world' at large. Nevertheless, a crucial difference remains between the church and the sect at this level: the latter can, in principle, reject society's attitude towards war, whereas the former cannot. For the church to remain a church, it cannot repudiate society at large on this issue, at least not actually during time of warfare.

There is, of course, a sociological danger inherent in this final approach to establishing the social determinants of just-war theories. The latter are treated as both partial symptoms and differentia of churches as distinct from sects. Thus, a just-war

42

theory is identified, in part at least, as one of the products of a church-type of religious organisation, but it is also used as one of the distinguishing marks between a church and a sect. Such confusion is perhaps inevitable, given the sharp differences between sociologists as to which criteria are most applicable to Church/Sect typology. Nevertheless, whatever typologies are ultimately adopted, an important difference between the pre- and post-Constantinian churches can be seen, both from the perspective of their social structure and from that of their theological beliefs, including those relating to war. Given this situation, it is important for the sociologist to attempt to correlate these differing structures and beliefs.

The sociologist, then, by examining aspects of theology from these three basic approaches—socio-cultural, socio-political and socio-ecclesiastical—can hope to uncover some of the social determinants of theology. In so far as he does this, he is undertaking an important part of a sociological account of theology.

3

Determinants in the Churches' Responses to Abortion

In the previous chapter I sought to provide a theoretical framework for studying the social determinants of theology. I suggested three levels of analysis—socio-cultural, socio-political and socio-ecclesiastical—and then attempted to relate them to the specific issue of theological responses to the ethical problem of war. The present chapter will form a more extended analysis of another issue, namely, the social determinants involved in the churches' varying responses to abortion. It too will use the same three-fold analytical framework.

It should be stressed at once that such sociological analysis will not be able to prescribe future theology or action for the churches. Sociological description must not be confused with theological or ethical prescription.[1] The 'is', 'was', 'will be' or 'could be' of the first are quite different from the second's 'ought to be' or 'should be'.[2] The most that the churches can expect from such analysis is a more critical awareness of their own role.[3]

Religious Affiliation and Abortion:
However, the attempt to analyse the social determinants of the churches' responses to abortion faces an initial difficulty. The little sociological research that has been done in this area, suggests that religion tends to act as an independent, rather than as a dependent, variable in society. More specifically, it appears that religious affiliation acts as a more powerful indicator of an individual's attitude towards abortion than most other social variables.

Two surveys in a western state of North America seem to confirm this suggestion.[4] The authors, Richardson and Fox, attempted to analyse the legislative voting on abortion reform bills presented in 1967, 1969 and 1971. The state that they chose was particularly interesting, because its legislators consisted of a high percentage of Catholics, Protestants and Mormons. Predicting favourable voting on abortion reform only from the Protestants, they found that, in the lower house voting:

> The only variable that consistently allowed prediction of voting behaviour is religious affiliation. Age never aided in predicting, and even decreased the ability to predict in all the sessions. Party also decreased the ability to predict voting behaviour. Constituency helped to predict only in 1969, though at a low level. The pattern for religious affiliation, although varied, was always positive.[5]

Their findings for the state senate voting behaviour were similar.

Of particular interest in the present context is that the authors made their prediction from a study of the relevant theological beliefs of Catholics, Protestants and Mormons. They argued that Catholic, as distinct from Protestant, theology opposes abortion on the grounds that a human being exists from the moment of conception, thus making abortion an act of murder. Mormon theology on this issue is more complex however:

> All human beings come into existence in a premortal or pre-earth stage. They do not possess a physical body; however, they do have intelligence and can (and do) exercise free will during this premortal existence. They are spirit children of God, who has created them individually to lead unique and purposeful lives. In order to achieve the postearth life or heavenly state of shared existence with God, the spirit children must elect to be born into earth life or mortal existence. Therefore, birth is viewed as a transition stage from pre-earth to earth life. Anything that interferes with this transition is of course condemned, and abortion is simply viewed as the murder of a spirit child who is seeking to make his way to postlife existence. Those involved in an abortion, for whatever reason, are held responsible for the soul of the individual who is kept from earthly existence (and therefore future heavenly existence) by the abortion.[6]

The possibility exists, though, that such theological notions may have little effect on Mormon legislators. The authors admit that 'it is possible that Catholics and Mormons may respond less to their ostensible theological beliefs, and more to the authority structures of their respective churches'.[7] If this were the case, then the possibility of theology acting as an independent variable within this situation is taken one stage further back. Those who wish to defend such a possibility must claim that theology has influenced the Catholic and Mormon Churches' official positions and the latter have in turn influenced their adherents.

It is certainly noticeable that this and other[8] studies of the relation between religion and attitudes and responses to abortion tend to rely on the weakest of the indicators of religious practice, that of religious affiliation. One of the problems involved in using the latter as a serious guide to the social significance of theology is that it gives no indication of either the strength or the sophistication of people's religious beliefs. Thus, to be a 'Protestant' in the survey one might never go to church, pray, believe or even know many of the central theological tenets of one's elected denomination.

Shifts in Ecclesiastical Attitudes to Abortion

The claim that it is the churches' official positions themselves which are determined solely by theological considerations is undermined by even the briefest historical examination. Such examination would suggest that the Roman Catholic Church has made a number of changes in its official reaction to abortion and that these changes continue and also, that the Protestant Churches have seen a number of radical changes. Taken together, an overview of these changes suggests the strong possibility that it is as much society which effects them as theology. This claim does not, of course, rule out the possibility *tout court* that theological concepts exercise an influence on Catholic and Protestant official ecclesiastical positions: it suggests only that they are by no means the sole influence.

It is well known that the mediaeval Catholic Church distinguished between the quickened and unquickened foetus, tending only to view an abortion of the former as culpable homicide. For a time, the church even followed the Aristotelian distinction between the date of animation of the male and

47

female foetus, believing that the first occurs up to the fortieth day after conception and the second up to the eightieth day. Whilst this distinction was eventually found to be impracticable[9] (since it is obviously difficult to determine gender before an abortion), that between an animated and unanimated foetus was not refuted by implication until 1869, when Pius IX affirmed that the ensoulment of the foetus commences at conception and set excommunication as the penalty for those seeking to procure an abortion.[10]

Despite the long history of the distinction within the church between an animated and an unanimated foetus, a more rigorous attitude apparently prevailed in the early church. Amongst the Primitive Fathers, Minucius, Felix and Tertullian all condemned abortion without distinction. Further, the Council of Elvira (c. 300) in the West, decreed that a woman guilty of an abortion be refused Holy Communion, even on her death-bed:[11] and the Synod of Ancyra (314) in the East, ordained a penalty of ten years 'penance for the woman who had an abortion.[12] However, by Augustine's time the distinction had arisen.

In the light of the discussion at the end of the previous chapter, this shift that occurred with Augustine might be expected. From the sociological perspective, it seems possible that the socio-political and socio-cultural changes that were taking place in the Roman world, allied to the new-found status of the church, necessitated a less rigorous response to this ethical issue. From this perspective, it was by no means as important an issue as that concerning war. The latter, as a crucial and topical issue of public morality, clearly raised fundamental questions about the relation between church and state. Nevertheless, as an issue concerning all citizens, whether overtly Christian or not, it was still important: an over-sectarian response by a church on such an issue might jeopardise its social status as a church.

By the nineteenth century, such social pressures may have been felt less keenly by the Roman Catholic Church. Besides, medical and physiological advances had rendered the mediaeval distinction less tenable. Certainly decrees of 1884, 1889, 1902, 1930 and 1968 all without exception condemned abortion. That of 1902 condemned abortion in respect of ectopic gestation, whilst the encyclical *Casti Conubii* of Pius XI in 1930 decreed that the life of the unborn child is as sacred as that of the mother and Paul VI's encyclical *Humanae Vitae* in 1968 condemned abortion even for therapeutic reasons.

In complete contrast to the response of the same church to the ethical issue of war, it would seem that it *is* possible for a church whilst still remaining a church, to maintain a position out of favour with public opinion on an issue of private morality such as abortion or contraception. However, whilst there is some truth in this claim, it misses two vital pieces of evidence.

First, it is possibly only in the last few years that public opinion has increasingly come to support the legitimacy of limited abortion reform. Whilst the opinion polls that have been held in Britain are notoriously unreliable, using different sampling techniques and types of question, a comparison at just two points might be indicative. A National Opinion Poll of 2000 electors in 1965 suggested that 24 per cent were totally opposed to abortion, whereas a Gallup Poll sample of 1,000 stratified interviewees in 1969 (i.e. *after* the implementation on the Abortion Act 1967) gave only 13 per cent and an Opinion Research Centre Poll of 982 electors in 1971 gave 6 per cent men and 9 per cent women. Conversely, the 1965 NOP suggested that 6 per cent were in favour of abortion on request, whereas the 1969 Gallup gave 18 per cent and the 1971 ORC 20 per cent men and 15 per cent women.[13] A shift in public opinion might cautiously be suggested from these figures.

More significantly, perhaps, it would appear that there is a fairly generalised trend within the West towards 'liberalised' abortion legislation. Within Europe alone, the last decade has witnessed a startling change. In the early 1960s, European countries which legally permitted abortion on social or psychological grounds were markedly in the minority: by the mid-1970s, it is those countries which do not legally permit such abortions that are in the minority.[14] Naturally there is no necessary correlation between social legislation and public opinion. Nevertheless, on an issue which involves so many people so directly some degree of correlation might be expected. On *a priori* grounds at least, it would seem that there has been some sort of shift in public opinion towards abortion law reform

—whether the latter results from, or causes, this shift need not be settled here.

Secondly, it is arguable that there is a shift taking place in the official response of the Roman Catholic Church itself to abortion. Superficially, the decrees already cited suggest that the church has maintained its absolutist position of 1869. Other indications, albeit small ones, might suggest that it has not. Currently, the removal of an ectopic pregnancy may be considered licit, as might the sacrifice of a foetus when this is incidental to and not the main purpose of, an operation to excise a diseased organ.[15] Further, some authorities allow for dilatation and curettage within a very few days after a case of rape, on the supposition that conception may not have yet taken place.[16] These exceptions are certainly small, but once they are allied to the known fact that some Roman Catholic women, even whilst remaining practising Catholics, do make use of the contraceptive and abortive facilities offered by the state,[17] they may provide the sociologist with evidence that the official response of the church to abortion is changing once again.

Certainly, a changing response to contraception and abortion, closely correlated with changes in public opinion, is evident within many non-Roman Catholic churches in the West. The Church of England, in particular, furnishes an excellent example of such change and the social determinants that are responsible for it. The ready availability of its public pronouncements on these twin issues makes it an obvious candidate for sociological analysis—although, in fact, many other churches might have been examined instead.

The Lambeth Conference of Anglican bishops of 1908 condemned the practice of contraception as 'demoralising to character and hostile to national welfare'. The 1920 Conference suggested that it would 'threaten the race' and that 'the teaching which, under the name of science and religion, encourages married people in the deliberate cultivation of sexual union as an end in itself' should be opposed. The 1930 Conference, however, allowed that, whilst the 'primary and obvious' method of limiting parenthood, where there was a 'clearly felt moral obligation' to do so, was 'complete abstinence from intercourse', *other methods* might be used, 'provided that this is done in the light of' Christian principles. Such motives as 'selfishness, luxury, or mere convenience' were considered to be inadequate. By 1958 the same Conference asserted that God had laid the primary responsibility for deciding upon 'the number and frequency of children' upon parents everywhere, but it left the means of such planning to their own 'positive choice before God'.[18]

Having reviewed this evidence from the Lambeth Conferences, G. R. Dunstan claims that it represents an important insight into the formulation of Christian ethics:

> The Lambeth Conference of 1958 did no more—and no less— than reduce into the terms of a resolution (with supporting argument elsewhere) a moral judgement already made, tested and acted upon by Christian husbands and wives, episcopal and clerical as well as lay, for years before; they had, despite ecclesiastical discouragement, admitted contraception into their married life and could not convict themselves of sin in having done so. The importance of the 1958 Report and Resolution, therefore, is that it exemplifies an instance in which the *magisterium* of the church formulated and ratified a moral judgement made by a sort of *consensus fidelium*, for which a good theological justification was worked out *ex post facto*.[19]

Whatever the merits of this claim in the context of Christian ethics, from the sociological perspective it tends to ignore the evidence suggesting that, on this issue, theology acted as a dependent variable and society as the independent variable. It seems clear, not only that the 1958 Resolution followed a change in public opinion, but that members of the Church of England themselves were already adhering to this opinion, rather than to the earlier Lambeth Resolutions. At the socio-cultural level of analysis, it is difficult to resist the conclusion that the church's changing position was socially determined: theology operated *ex post facto* must lack some social significance.

On the specific issue of abortion, an even more startling change is evident within the Church of England—and also within many other non-Roman Catholic churches in the West. From a situation at the beginning of the century, in which its official response to abortion would have differed very little from

51

that of the Roman Catholic Church, in 1965 it produced a report supporting limited abortion reform.

The report of the Church of England's Board for Social Responsibility recommended that British law on abortion should be changed. Placing the emphasis solely upon the women seeking an abortion—and not upon the state of the foetus—it suggested that the legal ground for abortion should be based on 'grave risk of the patient's death or serious injury to her health or physical or mental well-being', taking into account 'the patient's total environment, actual or reasonably forseeable'.[20]

A full examination of the role of the Church of England's response to abortion in the British context, would obviously be too parochial in an analysis of the social determinants of the churches' response to abortion. Nevertheless, two points are particularly pertinent and, at the same time capable of a rather wider reference. These suggest that the Church of England's changed response to abortion owed much to societal pressures of which it was largely unaware at the time.

First, it is clear that the report of 1965 believed that its particular recommendations would alter the *status quo* within Britain very little. Thus it admits:

> The humane reader will by this time be aware—as the members of the Committee are aware—that, so far as the law is concerned, the result of these deliberations would be to leave the substance of the law little changed, though the actual terms employed to give effect to the law's intention might be changed considerably.[21]

In effect, the report believed that its recommendations simply brought the law into line with established case-law in England and Wales and actual law in Scotland. In itself this alteration of the law would not drastically affect the rate of legal abortions in Britain.

This belief seems to have been shared by others within the church at the same time. An examination of the pastoral care literature within Britain at this period suggests that few anticipated the fact that a change in the abortion law would result in a great increase of legal abortions. Certainly Kenneth Child's book *Sick Call*, although it specifically refers to the Church of

England's report, devotes little space to the pastoral care of those confronted with abortion. Further, of the space that it does devote to this subject, most is concerned with women confronted with illegal abortion.[22]

Secondly, it is arguable in retrospect that had the Church of England's recommendations been accepted in full, they would in fact have resulted in a considerable increase in legal abortions in Britain. The actual grounds adopted in the Abortion Act 1967 were as follows:

(a) that the continuance of the pregnancy would involve risk to the life of the pregnant woman, or of injury to the physical or mental health of the pregnant woman or any existing children of her family, greater than if the pregnancy were terminated; or

(b) that there is a substantial risk that if the child were born it would suffer from such physical or mental abnormalities as to be seriously handicapped.[23]

Clearly these grounds are considerably more flexible than those suggested by the Church of England—allowing for the foetus to be considered as well as the woman and making no mention of 'grave' risk to the latter. Nevertheless, it is evident now that the vast majority of abortions are performed on the basis of the mental health of the woman[24]—a ground allowed for, albeit in a somewhat different form, in the Church of England's report. Further, the different wording of mental health grounds elsewhere in Europe would appear to have little effect on rates of legal abortions.[25] Arguably, it is a change in the law which is the operative factor, not the minutiae of the particular wording adopted. Certainly, in the British context, English and Scottish law were sufficiently problematic before the implementation of the Abortion Act to discourage any widespread use of abortion or any establishment of private nursing homes catering for legal abortions. After 1967 the situation changed radically; the English and Welsh no longer had to rely on case-law and the Scots could be more certain of the status of their law. Conceivably, almost *any* act allowing for abortion on mental or social grounds could have produced this situation—even one based on the Church of England's recommendations.

If this argument is accepted, it is evident that members of

the Church of England were themselves unaware of the potential effects of their proposals. The subsequent uneasiness amongst some of its representatives about the working of the Abortion Act in Britain would again suggest that this is the case,[26] as would a number of Governmental submissions made by the Board of Social Responsibility on the subject.[27]

To the sociologist, however, this pattern of absolute prohibition of abortion, followed by a limited acceptance of abortion, followed by proposals for legal reform and then doubts about the effects of a partial implementation of this reform, would suggest that it is not entirely explicable in theological terms. Undoubtedly, theological considerations *were* espoused even whilst members of the Church of England were changing their response to abortion. Nevertheless, their social determination is apparent, as it is indeed in the following quotation from the 1965 report:

> We have to assert, as normative, the general inviolability of the foetus: to defend, as a first principle, its right to live and develop; and then to lay the burden of proof to the contrary firmly on those who, in particular cases, would wish to extinguish that right on the ground that it was in conflict with another or others with a higher claim to recognition. Only so, in fact, can we maintain the *intention* of the moral tradition, which is to uphold the value and importance of human life. For invariably in this discussion the question must arise, which life? And the absolutist adherence to a refusal of abortion *in all circumstances* might well result, in some, in a frustration of that intention.[28]

It is possible that this passage, too, is an *ex post facto* theological justification of an existing situation within British society. At the time, a limited amount of legal abortions was allowed, although there were already strong pressures to change the law in order to allow for more. Whilst the Church of England's report was unwilling to comply fully with the latter, it is apparent from this quotation that it was prepared to legitimate the former. So, despite an apparent emphasis upon the 'right to life' of the foetus—as in the contemporary Roman Catholic tradition—the report *was* prepared to make significant qualifications in terms of the 'general' inviolability of the foetus and the 'intention' of the moral tradition. It even sought to strengthen this *ex post facto* position with an attack on 'absolutist' stances on the issue of abortion.

Interestingly, Dunstan criticised the British Abortion Act precisely because it responded to public opinion. Having reviewed the changes that took place in the draft Bill as it passed through Parliament—changes that, as he argued, thoroughly distorted the Church of England's proposals (in which he himself took part)—he claimed:

> It would appear, therefore, that the tendency of the ethics of justifiable feticide which I have sketched here runs directly contrary to the tide of practice, not only in Britain but all over the world. The facts of the incidence of induced abortion invite only one conclusion: that abortion is now being more widely legalised and practised because that is what people want—an indication for medical intervention for the destruction of life unknown in our ethics before.[29]

In terms of the analysis I am suggesting, the argument contained in this quotation misses two crucial points. First, the Church of Englands' own position, as expressed in the 1965 report, would itself appear to be determined by public opinion. Both in its seeking to provide a theological justification of the *status quo* and in offering concrete proposals in the form of a draft Bill on abortion, a degree of social determination would appear to be present in the report. Secondly, in so far as the Church of England's proposals might have produced a similar effect to that of the actual legislation adopted, they might be regarded as more inherently in tune with public opinion than even their authors realised at the time. Not only was the Church of England apparently legitimating the contemporary situation within society at large, it was also providing for a radically changed situation in the future. Curiously, the proposals of an ostensibly theologically motivated report would appear to have been doubly determined, reflecting directly both the *status quo* and the *status quo post*.

As the existing legislation prohibiting abortion in all but the most exceptional circumstances is gradually changed throughout Europe and the United States[30] (the Supreme Court decision in 1973 effecting a very rapid change indeed in the latter), examples of *ex post facto* theological justification can be found in many of the non-Roman Catholic churches. Whilst the issue of abortion has caused more opposition amongst the churches to state legislation than any similar legislation on a matter of public morality (such as war), a discernible shift is apparent within most churches. Even the position of the Roman Catholic Church has not remained static.

Correlates Between Theology and Action:

My analysis to this point would seem to confirm the overall thesis that there are discernible social determinants in the churches' responses to abortion. Whilst, in some instances at least, religious affiliation may remain an important variable in determining people's attitudes towards abortion (though perhaps not always their actual behaviour[31]), the official theological positions of many churches may owe much to general public opinion. In Britain, at least (and elsewhere, too, although this cannot be demonstrated here), it would seem that the latter increasingly favours a more widespread use of abortion than in the past. Given that this is the situation, then the evident changes within the Church of England during this century and the possible changes within the contemporary Roman Catholic Church, may well be closely correlated with this changing public opinion.

In terms of my three levels of sociological analysis, an overview of these two churches' responses to abortion produces a fairly comprehensive pattern of social determinants. Without attempting an exhaustive survey of all existing ecclesiastical responses to abortion, or even an ideal typification of all possible responses, a comparison of these two churches alone suggests an interesting array of societal influences.

At the socio-cultural level of analysis, the close correspondence between public opinion and ecclesiastical response would appear significant. This is most evident, of course, in the case of the Church of England. On the available evidence, it would seem that both its absolutist rejection of abortion and contraception at the beginning of the century and its gradual acceptance of them both up to 1967, accorded with public opinion within Britain at these times. Only after the radical changes affected by the Abortion Act 1967 did the views of officials within the

Church of England possibly differ significantly from those within society in general. Even here it is possible that opinions are shifting again within the Church of England—despite an initial rejection by all but one of the bishops of the Abortion Bill in the House of Lords.[32]

Within the Roman Catholic Church the situation is more complex, since it is evidently radically opposed to current legislation on abortion in Britain. The Aristotelian distinction between the animated and unanimated foetus adopted by the mediaeval Catholic Church and retained (with a short interruption from 1588 to 1591) until the mid-nineteenth century, may, however, be an indication that it has not always rejected public opinion. This distinction enabled the church to tolerate a measure of early abortion, without necessarily having to condone it. Even in the current situation, there are indications (albeit small ones) that the absolutist rejections of contraception and abortion of the nineteenth and early twentieth centuries, are being modified. Clearly, in the instance of contraception, *Humanae Vitae* criticised the means, rather than the fact, of birth control, but even on the issue of abortion a less than absolutist position is apparent.

At the socio-political level of analysis, the role of the Church of England on the issue of abortion is again interesting. Its response to the political realities of the 1960s was largely shaped by those realities. Thus, instead of campaigning for the *status quo* within Britain (which most nearly represented its own position) it was prompted to offer draft legislation. Whilst largely unaware of the likely effects of its own legislative proposals, as I have argued, it was nevertheless prepared to offer them. As a result, far from determining the shape of the actual legislation passed, the Church of England found that it was apparently legitimating grounds for abortion which it did not support.[33] Political realities accordingly did have a determinative effect on the church's proposals.

On the other hand, the political response of the Roman Catholic Church within countries allowing legal abortions has been quite different. Far from offering draft legislation, many churches have participated in political lobbies to change existing laws. Seldom, indeed, have churches campaigned so

57

consistently and actively on a matter of moral/political importance. Further, for those confronted with an unwanted pregnancy, there have been a variety of attempts to set up counselling and caring organisations offering 'alternatives to abortion'.[34] In contrast to those non-Roman Catholic churches, who support varying degrees of legal abortion, but yet seldom offer facilities for the pastoral care of those confronted with abortion, the Roman Catholic Church has been significantly active.[35] Whilst responding to given political realities—and thus showing a clear determination by them—this church has actively sought to challenge them.

Finally, at the level of socio-ecclesiastical analysis, both churches again suggest determinants involved in their particular responses to abortion. A thoroughgoing sectarian response is evident only in the earliest phase of the Catholic Church, that is in its pre-Constantinian period. Its initial absolutist rejection of abortion would have accorded ill with opinion in the surrounding Roman Empire: just as the church could afford to have a thoroughgoing pacifist orientation at this time, so it could reject the 'pagan' custom of abortion. Significantly, the distinction between an animated and an unanimated foetus was adopted after Constantine—that is, after the church's change in status from a sect-type to a church-type orientation. Likewise, the 'established' Church of England's response to abortion apparently differs little from that of public opinion within Britain. Only the contemporary Roman Catholic Church appears to differ from society at large on this issue—and even it may be changing.

Prior ethical responses to abortion, then—themselves dependent on observable social determinants—would seem to be correlated with differing pastoral activities in the area of abortion-care. A complex pattern of social causation begins to emerge; pastoral action in the churches may be influenced by theologico-ethical beliefs, which in turn might be influenced by public opinion, which in turn may be influenced by legislation, which is supposedly influenced by public opinion, which. . . . Further, this pattern is made considerably more complex by the introduction of an interactionist approach, taking seriously the possibility that specifically theological ideas may be socially significant as well as socially determined within this situation. Indeed, the foregoing analysis of the responses of the churches to those confronted with abortion would seem, at times, to require such an analysis. The particular and differing theologico-ethical responses of the churches, once constructed, become social realities and possibly socially significant realities. Thus, to a particular Roman Catholic priest it matters little that his church's official position is socially determined: it none the less exists and his pastoral response to a woman seeking an abortion must take it into account.

This complex tangle of social interactions gives both sociologist and theologian much to contemplate. The fact that abortion creates ambivalence and anxiety within both the churches and society at large, may give them added incentive. From a position of relative detachment, it demonstrates well the difficulties facing any application of the sociology of knowledge to theology.

4

The Social Significance of Theology

IF FEW sociologists of religion have studied the social determinants of theology, still fewer have studied its social significance. The discipline is seldom treated as anything other than epiphenomenal and the symbols and concepts it generates are usually ignored in sociological accounts of contemporary religiosity. Even detailed accounts of differing religious organisations pay scant attention to theological variables.

Nevertheless, an analysis of the social structure of theology must take seriously the possibility that theology may at times be socially significant. More specifically, it must be prepared to explore the claim that theological ideas (even viewed as social constructions) once generated, may have an influence upon society at large. It will be the function of this chapter and the next to explore this claim.

There are at least two reasons why contemporary sociologists of religion have tended to ignore the possibility that theology may act at times as an independent variable within society. The first depends upon viewing it in the context of a process of secularisation. Amongst those sociologists who have advanced a thoroughgoing secularisation model,[1] there has been a tendency to view contemporary theology as both the product and the victim of secularisation. Together with a number of theologians,[2] they have argued that theological movements like that of secular theology, or even ecumenical theology,[3] are themselves a part of the process of secularisation, contributing directly to the demise of the discipline as a whole. In addition (and somewhat paradoxically), they argued that, within a situation of radical secularisation, theology has effectively ceased to be an influence upon society.

61

The second reason why contemporary sociologists have tended to ignore this possibility involves a more general scepticism about the social efficacy of intellectual ideas. Those sociologists of knowledge, like Berger and Luckmann,[4] who stress the social significance of everyday knowledge, tend at the same time to denigrate the significance of intellectual knowledge. Thus, specifically intellectualistic disciplines like theology are regarded as socially epiphenomenal—even when, as in the instance of Berger,[5] they are considered to be intrinsically interesting.

Once it is admitted that both of these arguments depend upon debatable assumptions, the sociologist of religion can no longer be excused for his comparative ignorance of theology. If it is conceded that the secularisation model in its most radical form, does less than justice to the ambiguity of contemporary religion and that intellectual ideas may yet be socially significant, an adequate sociological understanding of theology must take seriously the possibility that it may act as both a dependent and an independent variable within society. A genuinely interactionist approach to theology becomes a sociological imperative.

Nevertheless, the sociologist of religion can assume too easily that various theological movements and concepts are indeed socially significant. It is one thing to allow for the possibility that theology may act at times as an independent variable, but quite another to demonstrate that particular features of the discipline actually influence specific social situations. Amongst those few contemporary sociologists of religion who have considered the social function of theology, a too facile jump is made from this general possibility to an actual demonstration. The works of Roger Mehl in France and M. J. Jackson in Britain well illustrate this danger.

Even though he recognises the importance of an examination of the social determinants of theology, Mehl maintains that 'the common error of the sociologist is that of thinking that he does not have to take doctrinal elements into consideration, because these elements would be the intellectual superstructures which only record a religion's effort to adapt to the cultural level in which it lives'.[6] In contrast to other socio-

62

logists, Mehl insists that particular attention must be paid to the role of theology, if one is to understand Protestantism:

> If a sociology of Christianity must take account of this fact, a sociology of Protestantism has even more reason to bear it in mind. For Protestantism was born of a doctrinal reform which was effected by doctors of theology. This reform was raised against the omnipotence of practices, of forms of piety, of the elements of sociological morphology. It aspired to reform the visible communities of the church according to a doctrinally determined archetype. It had desired that the line going from Christology through ecclesiology to the organisation of the parishes be as direct as possible. The question is not primarily one of knowing if the Reformation was perfectly successful in this enterprise and if 'non-theological factors' intervened in the constitution of the church and of the parishes. The primary obligation of the sociologist who studies the Protestant church is that of taking account of this intention, of this essence of Protestantism, following which he can investigate the manner in which they have operated or not operated.[7]

This quotation is attractive, since it apparently confirms the suggestion that theology is socially significant. None the less, it is open to criticism at a number of points. The sociologist of religion may feel that there is nothing in Protestantism, rather than Catholicism, which especially obliges him to take theology more or less seriously. Further, he might maintain that it is precisely the exploration of 'non-theological factors' within both Protestantism and Catholicism which constitutes the most interesting and original part of his study. In such exploration, the sociologist, as a sociologist, has been able to make his most important contribution to the study of religion as a whole. And finally, the sociologist may feel less than happy with Mehl's apparently extra-sociological depiction of the 'essence' of Protestantism. After all, Mehl himself rejects the idea elsewhere that sociology should imagine that 'it reaches religion in its essence'.[8]

A similar, unsubstantiated jump, from the general possibility to the actuality of the social significance of theology, is apparent in the work of M. J. Jackson. His analysis of the relation between sociology and theology begins with and centres upon, theology as an independent variable within society. Thus, he reviews at some length Karl Barth's apparent rejection of 'religion' and natural theology, in favour of 'revelation' through Jesus Christ and Hans Küng's 'Christian universalism', following Vatican II's *Constitution on the Church*. Of the latter, especially, Jackson argues that, in relation to world religions, 'the dangers of relativism are . . . apparent, as also danger of an end to dialogue, for why bother to talk if we are all going the same way to the same destination?'[9] Barth's attitude towards 'religion' led to the whole-hearted missionary activity of men like Hendrik Kraemer, whereas Küng's 'universalism' tended to relax 'the urge to mission'.[10]

In the light of this analysis, Jackson argues strongly for the social significance of theology, seen as 'the understanding and explanation of the religious dimension of life':[11]

> The views of the theologian about religion are of the first importance to the sociology of religion. What the theologians say about religion has considerable impact on the belief and practice of religious bodies, on how their members see their functions, on how religious bodies relate themselves to the outside world, on their programmes of mission, on their attitudes to other religions. The views . . . of Barth and Küng, of quasi-rejection and acceptance of religion, are widely held and full of practical implications.[12]

Unfortunately, Jackson's thesis is stated rather than argued. The differing theological responses of these two theologians to 'religion' may well be socially significant beyond the bounds of the theological world itself, but no evidence is given to demonstrate this. *A priori*, an end to dialogue is not the only possible response to Küng's 'universalism' and in practice Barthianism may or may not be dominant amongst active missionaries. A more sophisticated analysis is essential, if the possibility of theology acting as an independent variable within society is to be firmly established.

Yet, if this is established, then it will clearly be of interest to both theologians and sociologists of religion. Theologians may be heartened to know that their work has an influence beyond a small religious elite: sociologists of religion may be forced to take the work of theologians more seriously, whatever they might otherwise think of its validity. Alternatively, theologians may be somewhat dismayed at the unintended consequences of their writings, whilst sociologists become even more convinced than ever of the epiphenomenal nature of the specifically religious content of these writings. In either instance, a study of the social significance of theology would be important.

It is worth stressing, *en passant*, that, despite the obvious attractions of such a study for the theologian, the sociologist, as a sociologist, may at times explore possibilities which are apparently harmful to the theological enterprise. Jackson argues that a sociologist of religion should ideally be a believer, since 'neutrality' *vis-à-vis* religion is impossible and the believer 'enters religion sympathetically'.[13] Not only would most other sociologists see this as a dangerous dictum,[14] but they might also claim that Jackson's own attempt to defend theology as an independent variable is itself theologically, rather than sociologically, motivated.[15] If the sociologist is to examine theology adequately, he cannot be under continuous pressure from the theologian.[16] Rather, like the critical biblical scholar or philosopher of religion, even within a theological faculty, he is obliged to pursue the consequences of his discipline wherever they might lead and 'as if' it were the only relevant discipline.[17] If this were not the case, then the possible correlations between certain types of theology and anti-Semitism[18] or racism[19] might never have been investigated. It is worth recalling one of Max Weber's footnotes to his *The Protestant Ethic and the 'Spirit 'of Capitalism:*

> From theologians I have received numerous valuable suggestions in connection with this study. Its reception on their part has been in general friendly and impersonal, in spite of wide differences of opinion on particular points. This is the more welcome to me since I should not have wondered at a certain antipathy to the manner in which these matters must necessarily be treated here. What to a theologian is valuable in his religion cannot play a very large part in this study. We are concerned with what, from a religious point of view, are often quite superficial and unrefined aspects of religious life, but which, and precisely because they are superficial and unrefined, have often influenced outward behaviour most profoundly.[20]

Theology as an Independent Variable:

In contrast to the contemporary neglect of theology by sociologists of religion, two of the pioneers of the discipline took it more seriously. The theologian Ernst Troeltsch and the sociologist Max Weber were prepared to treat, not only religion, but also theology, as an independent variable within society: for both, specifically theological symbols and concepts were socially significant. Further, major elements in their contributions towards a sociological understanding of religion would be negated if the possibility were removed of theology acting as an independent variable within society. If, for this reason alone, the comparative neglect of this area by sociologists today must appear strange.

The small amount of research that does exist in this area tends to be clustered around the Weberian thesis and the post-Troeltsch Church/Sect typology. The first tends to examine continuing differences between Catholics and Protestants, based on their supposed theological differences, while the second tends to differentiate churches, denominations and sects, at least partially, on their varying theological responses to each other and to the world at large. However, with the exception of the research discussed in the previous chapter and that to be discussed in the next, few sociologists indeed have explored new ways in which theology may be socially significant.

Weber's own thesis, contained in *The Protestant Ethic and the 'Spirit' of Capitalism*, is too well known to be reviewed in detail here. Starting, as it did, from the empirical observations that business leaders and owners of capital within the West tended to be Protestant rather than Catholic and that Benjamin Franklin's self-acknowledged ethic involved 'the earning of more and more money, combined with the strict avoidance of all spontaneous enjoyment of life',[21] Weber suggested that one of the cultural factors enabling capitalism to arise in the West may have been Calvinist theology. Inevitably, the specific correlation that Weber sought to demonstrate between the Protestant doctrines of the calling, predestination, asceticism and sanctification and the 'spirit' of Western European and American capitalism is a complex one. Had it not been, it would scarcely have received so much attention from the academic community.

But, just as inevitably, it has been subjected to considerable criticism,[22] which again need not be reviewed here. Several methodological points, however, are of immediate interest: in addition, all have been overlooked, at times, in the research that the thesis has generated.

First, Weber consistently maintained that theology was just one variable involved in the rise of capitalism within the West. Other factors, such as rational book-keeping, transport, etc., were equally, if not more, important. The modest role he adopted for his thesis was 'to ascertain whether and to what extent religious forces have taken part in the qualitative formation and the quantitative expansion' of the spirit of Capitalism over the world:[23] he made no claim that capitalism could never have arisen without the Reformation or that the latter was the sole cause of the former. Whilst he treated certain theological ideas as being socially significant, he never suggested that they were exclusively significant.

This point must be fundamental to any attempt to study the social significance of theology. Exaggerated claims about the extent of this significance, unsupported by rigorous empirical evidence, can play no part in it. So, for example, Kevin Clement's important claim that, following the Depression in New Zealand, theological considerations were socially significant, must be set in the context which he analyses. In the period 1925–31, he suggests, the churches tacitly and explicitly accepted the *status quo*: in the period 1931–4 they 'started developing social teaching that stood in radical contrast to earlier statements sympathetic to the maintenance of the *status quo*':[24] and only in the period 1934–5 did 'religious opinion leaders' adopt overtly radical political stances, giving considerable support to the Labour party and helping it to win the election in 1935 by providing it with a religious legitimation. Thus, he argues that, at first religious and theological factors operated only as dependent variables, but that by 1934 'the religious variable exerted considerable independent influence on social change, by legitimating the agents of change—the Labour Party—and by suggesting specific innovations that the Labour Party might adopt in order to bring about a specifically Christian solution to the problem . . . it was by producing religious symbols to interpret the situation that the religious institutions exerted an independent influence on the changes that occurred'.[25] Clements, then, claims a relatively modest role for theology in this situation—that of producing legitimating symbols—and that only on the basis of rigorous research.[26] To have claimed more would have been to go beyond the evidence.

Secondly, Weber was concerned with interpreted or 'popular' theology, not with theology as produced by academics. A not infrequent criticism of the 'Protestant Ethic' thesis is, that it provides a thoroughly distorted account of Calvinism, imputing to it an illegitimate conception of its doctrines of the calling, election and sanctification. So, it is maintained that neither Calvin nor Luther accepted these doctrines in the manner in which Weber depicted them. However, this criticism misses the point that Weber was more concerned with these doctrines, as they might have been perceived by followers of Calvin and Luther, than by the theologians themselves. If theology is to be considered socially significant, the way that it is perceived by non-theologians becomes a matter of great importance, but the way that it is perceived by the theologians themselves becomes a matter of only peripheral concern. If specific notions within Calvinism did indeed contribute to the rise of capitalism within the West, it must have been these notions, as generally perceived, rather than as originally intended, which had this effect.

A focus upon perceived, rather than academic, theology presents the sociologist with a somewhat daunting task. He must now distinguish four levels of analysis; theology amongst academic theologians (i.e. the traditional focus), theology amongst preachers who are seeking to communicate it, whether in writing or orally, to a non-theological audience, theology amongst church attenders and readers of literature written by these preachers and, finally, theology amongst those who neither attend church nor read religious literature with any degree of regularity. In terms of my original definition of theology, it is only at the first level and at the written part of the second that theology, strictly understood, is to be found. Accordingly, the oral part of the second and the whole of the third and fourth levels are concerned with the effects of theology rather than with theology itself. Precisely because they are oral rather than written, though, they are less accessible to the sociologist. Just as Weber was forced to speculate about the 'probable' ways in which theology would be popularly perceived, so the contemporary sociologist is often presented with the same intractable difficulty. I will return to this point in the next chapter, when I consider the four levels of reaction to *Honest to God*.

Finally, it is important to stress that Weber was concerned with the rise of capitalism, not with its continued maintenance. Following Lenski's[27] adaption of the thesis into a general hypothesis through which to examine contemporary differences between Catholics and Protestants, suggesting as it did that religious affiliation may indeed act as an independent variable within society (itself a significant finding, given the widespread indifference to the sociology of religion at the time he was writing), a considerable amount of research has continued to subject these possible differences to empirical examination. Yet, it should not be forgotten that this does constitute an adaption of Weber's own thesis.[28] The latter was, after all, concerned with the rise of capitalism. Weber suggested that its specific maintenance was effected through such general moral values as thrift and hard work, now detached from their original religious setting. Thus, contemporary Capitalism need owe nothing to contemporary religious affiliation: once effected the former can survive quite well without the latter. Similarly, in Clements' suggested correlation between religious symbols and political actualities, the contemporary Labour Party in New Zealand need have no special relationship with the contemporary churches there. The Labour Party, having received the religious legitimation offered by the churches and thus the respectability that it previously lacked (before 1934 members were often suspected of Communism), could continue to hold office with or without the blessing of the churches.

The fact that Weber's thesis is essentially an historical one, does raise difficulties for the sociologist. As subsequent critics of the thesis have found, it is difficult to test in any sufficiently empirical or rigorous manner. This difficulty is compounded by the two qualifications already given—i.e. that the thesis is only

69

concerned with one of many possible variables and that it is based upon perceived rather than academic theology. Ironically, Weber's sophistication as a sociologist, producing models that usually are carefully qualified, allied to his *verstehen* methodology, served to produce a thesis which many would maintain is neither verifiable nor falsifiable.[29] Nevertheless, it has proved to be of enduring interest to sociologists.

A very similar criticism might be made of Ernst Troeltsch's Church/Sect typology—the study of differing types and dynamics within religious institutions. It is clear that he believed that his three types of religious organisation—Churches, Sects and Mysticism—owed their existence to the structure of the Christian Gospel itself. Troeltsch consistently maintained (a feature often ignored by contemporary sociologists of religion),[30] that the roots of his typology lay within Christian theology. For him, then, theology was socially significant in so far as it served to create and maintain the triadic structure of organisational responses to it. I have argued elsewhere that it is precisely this theological basis to his typology which creates difficulties for the sociologist, since the latter usually wishes to maintain that Church/Sect typology ought to be applicable to religions other than Christianity alone and that a mixture of theological and social criteria is undesirable in rigorous research.[31]

Nevertheless, despite these difficulties, Troeltsch's typology, like Weber's 'Protestant Ethic' thesis, has continued to attract the attention of sociologists of religion. More crucially, in the present context, both provide examples of attempts to analyse the social significance of theology: both take seriously the possibility that theological concepts may act at times as an independent variable within society.

Theology and Pacifism:

As in Chapter 3, the first part of this chapter has been concerned with analysing the work of others in this largely neglected area of sociological study. However, in the remainder of this chapter and in the next, I must show how the social significance of theology might actually be investigated. I propose to do this by returning to theological responses to war and only then by offering an analysis of responses to *Honest to God*.

Since I intend to concentrate upon only one type of theo-logical response to war—that of thoroughgoing pacifism—it is important to define more exactly the range of possible responses. Four 'ideal' types might be isolated. Since they are 'ideal' rather than 'actual' types, it is not, of course, necessary to claim that they are all to be found in a pure form within existing groups in society, or even that considerable overlap is not to be found in such groups. They are intended, instead, to denote the theoretical range of possibilities in such a way that actual responses to war can be better classified and compared. Ideal typifications are at best heuristic devices: they are means for interpreting society, rather than direct observations from society. Understood in this way, then, the four ideal types of response to war are as follows:

(A) *Thoroughgoing Militarism*—understood as a willingness to fight anywhere, at any time and for any cause.

(B) *Selective Militarism*—understood as a willingness to fight when one's country, or another, declares that the cause is just.

(C) *Selective Pacifism*—understood as a willingness to fight only when one is convinced that the cause is just.

(D) *Thoroughgoing Pacifism*—understood as an unwillingness to fight anywhere, at any time and for any cause.

It is clear that these four ideal types concentrate upon the willingness and intention of the individual confronted with war and make no attempt to account for other variables within this situation. It is also clear that B and C differ from A and D in their inclusion of the concept of perceived justice. As a result the sort of just-war theories discussed in Chapter 2 apply only to them. The point of distinction between B and C lies in the fact that, in the first, it is the individual's country or even another country/organisation (this ambiguity is intentionally unre-solved), which decides on the justice of a particular cause, whereas, in the second, it is the individual himself who so decides.

Within most, if not all, Christian organisations only types B, C and D would be considered to be possible Christian responses to war. Only a non-idealistic mercenary, perhaps, would conform to type A and he finds few defenders within Christianity.

Bainton's three historical attitudes to warfare in Christian and pre-Christian thinking (to which I referred earlier) namely, the crusade, the just-war and pacifism,[32] can be seen to be included in types B, C and D, although these types are naturally somewhat broader and not entirely coincidental with them. In particular, the distinction between C and D, both defended at times as varieties of Christian pacifism, becomes more evident. In general, it is only the last type that will be considered here, although it must be admitted that, in practice, it may sometimes be hard to distinguish between C and D. So, for example, Bertrand Russell, in effect a clear instance of type D, in theory admitted to the futuristic possibility of legitimate violent sanctions in a situation of world-government and as a result would be classified as type C. A similar problem will be noted presently in the context of the Jehovah's Witnesses' response to war. Whilst admitting this difficulty in the exact classification of individual empirical instances of pacifism, it is none the less thoroughgoing pacifism which will form the focus of this analysis.

It is, perhaps, in thoroughgoing pacifism that the social significance of theology should be most apparent. In other Christian responses to war the views of the individual, or of the particular religious organisation, tend, by definition, to be coincidental with those of the state. Accordingly, it becomes extremely difficult to determine how far the formers' views are determined simply by the latter's, or how far they might also be determined by the legitimations offered by theological expressions of a just-war theory. By contrast, the thoroughgoing pacifist, whether as an individual or as a sect, represents a deviant type within either society in general or Christianity in particular. Numerically, at least, types B and C represent the majority Christian response to war: type D accounts only for a very small minority. Of course, as I suggested earlier, it is quite possible to propose social determinants even for this last type[33] —methodologically no response to war should be excluded from such analysis—but there is an *a priori* possibility here that theological positions, even when viewed as socially constructed realities, may have acted as independent variables. This possibility may be investigated at the level both of the individual

72

thoroughgoing pacifist theologian and of the thoroughgoing pacifist sect.

At the level of the individual thoroughgoing pacifist theologian, Charles Raven again provides an instructive example. Whatever social determinants may be isolated in causing him to change from types B or C to D during the 1920s, there is strong evidence to be found in his writings to suggest that specifically theological factors significantly affected the position he maintained from that time until his death in 1965. Amongst a series of books on Christian responses to war he even entitled one *The Theological Basis of Christian Pacifism*:[34] indeed, it is the attempt to provide such a basis which forms the focus of his other writings on the subject.

Raven constantly rejected a variety of social variables as the cause of his pacifism. Given the polemical nature of his books on the subject and the considerable criticism to which he was subjected, it is not surprising to find that, whereas he frequently admitted social determinants to the attitudes of some of his fellow pacifists, he was reluctant to admit their relevance to his own. Thus, he conceded that the movement towards pacifism in the 1920s in Britain 'was largely due to motives of which the Christian can only disapprove'.[35] Amongst these he suggested that it was 'disgust and fear, the accumulated effects of nervous exhaustion and disappointment', which were mainly responsible.[36] He constantly sought to disassociate himself from such emotional reactions to war, even to the extent of admitting that the latter could produce desirable moral characteristics in those participating in it.

The accuracy of Raven's analysis of the social determinants of pacifism is less important in the present context than the fact of his resolution to differentiate his own position from such determinants. In his self-estimation it was theological considerations which provided the *raison d'être* for his Christian pacifism and as a professional theologian he sought to communicate these as widely as possible in lectures, books, speeches and sermons.

On several occasions he sought to show that Christian pacifism is derivable from the doctrine of the Trinity. Thus, having argued that war is not to be condemned simply because it

involves killing, suffering and the destruction of material re-
sources, he maintained that it is to be so condemned for
theological reasons:

> War destroys the essential fellowship which exists and should
> be fostered between human beings as children of God and mem-
> bers one of another. . . . The Christian doctrine of God centres
> upon . . . the personal qualities symbolised by love and life and
> light. The doctrine of the Incarnation bears witness to the
> sanctity of personality as the unique medium capable of
> revealing the Son of God. The Holy Spirit is primarily manifested
> in the *koinonia*, the communion and community of believers,
> the blessed society which is the body of Christ. This primary
> tenet of our faith is outraged and blasphemed by war.[37]

However, whilst he often used this trinitarian formulation,
the primary basis for his Christian pacifism appears to have
been his christological and soteriological beliefs. He argued,
throughout his writings on the subject, that 'Christ by his Cross
presents to us his way of overcoming the sin of the world, and
in this form at least the mass of mankind and even of Christians
repudiate it'.[38] With G. H. C. Macgregor, Raven claimed that
the Gospels, Acts and the Epistles are incontrovertibly pacifist-
oriented[39] and that Christ emerges from them as 'the prince of
peace'.[40] An adequate understanding of christology, then,
necessitates a pacifist interpretation of Christ. Further, an
understanding of soteriology in terms of the *Imitatio Christi*,
seeing Christ as a representative figure for others and implying
'a real identification of the believer with his Lord', necessitates
pacifism for Christian disciples.[41] So, given these understandings
of christology and soteriology, he believed that 'the plain fact is
that the Church since the First Century and with few exceptions
has never, despite its protestations, taken Christ with complete
seriousness'.[42]

It is important to realise that, had Raven interpreted the
New Testament evidence on which he based his christology
differently—as just-war theorists tend to do[43]—his conclusions
might have been rather different. Again, had he not based his
understanding of soteriology on an *Imitatio Christi*, his pacifist
conclusions for Christians would not necessarily have followed,

even had he maintained his christological beliefs. Thus, on other interpretations of soteriology, it would be perfectly possible to argue, that the fact of Christ's pacifism does not necessarily entail pacifism for Christ's disciples. Both features of his theological argument, then, are crucial to his justification of Christian pacifism, whether as direct causes of this pacifism or simply as maintainers of it. In either instance, specifically theological concepts would be accorded a socially significant role in Raven's overall response to war.

Not surprisingly, then, a case can be made out to the effect that the ethical positions of particular theologians may be influenced directly by their theological concepts. A more detailed demonstration of how this is possible must wait until Chapter 6. This possibility on its own, however, might appear remarkably uninteresting to the sociologist of knowledge. Werner Stark, for example, would doubtless argue that such an analysis of Raven belongs properly to microsociology and accordingly cannot constitute a part of a sociology of knowledge.[44] Even if his argument is not accepted, it can be seen that interest in such analysis will be limited only to those already predisposed towards theology.

Much more interesting for the sociologist, is the possibility that Raven's theological arguments themselves were socially significant. That is, there is a possibility that, not only was Raven's response to war influenced by theology, but that his theological justification of this response was itself an influence upon others. It is important to study this possibility in terms of the four levels of analysis I have already suggested; namely theologians, preachers, listeners and outsiders.

As the Regius Professor of Theology at Cambridge and the author of twenty-five theological works on a wide variety of subjects, it is difficult to believe that Raven's theological justification of pacifism was not widely known to academic theologians. However unpopular these views and those on the ordination of women might have been amongst the ecclesiastical hierarchy, his theological justification of them was important, at least within the academic community. William Temple, then Archbishop of York, clearly thought them sufficiently important to be refuted publicly in *The Times* in 1935. Further, on various occasions,

Raven used a series of university lectures to promote his theological polemic against war, notably in the Halley Stewart Lecture of 1934 and in the Robert Treat Paine Lectures of 1950, delivered at Boston University, Union Theological Seminary and the University of Chicago. At the time, his views on pacifism may even have been rather better known amongst academics than his views on other areas within theology.

Undoubtedly, Raven himself thought it important that academics, as such, were concerned intellectually with the issue of pacifism. Against his numerous critics, he maintained, at one point, 'Lord Ponsonby, Lord Russell, Mr Aldous Huxley, Mr Gerald Heard, Mr Middleton Murry and the Bishop of Birmingham are men whose intellectual power is probably greater than that of any group in the public life of Britain. . . where they, each from his special angle, have vindicated pacifism, they deserve a fuller answer than the casual comment of ecclesiastics and statesmen'.[45]

Raven also believed that a specifically theological consideration of war might help theology itself to become relevant beyond academic circles. For many years he held 'the particular question of the Christian attitude toward war as the most urgent and the most representative of those problems' concerned with the relationship of belief to practice.[46] But he also held that a consideration of the problem might help theology to become more socially significant than it had been for a long time:

> Theologians' . . . work has been frustrated by the fact that it is regarded as academic and almost as irrelevant. Their fellow Christians, whose concern is rather to live out the faith as they have received it than to deepen their understanding of its meaning, will only discover a renewed appreciation of it by approaching it along the line of some concrete problem which demands solution. We have claimed that war is such a problem. To study it would do as much to enlighten and deepen and unify the thought of the Churches as to clear up the particular issue.[47]

Doubtless to enable this broadening of theology to take place, Raven deliberately wrote his books on pacifism in a popular style, generally avoiding theological jargon and academic references. He was even invited in 1942 to write the Bishop of London's Lent Book on the theme of peace.

A very slight study of the bookshelves of those who were already ministers during the 1930s, would suggest that Raven was indeed successful in communicating, at least at this second level. Indeed, he himself, as the author of widely selling books on pacifism and as public speaker and preacher on the subject, was a part of this level of communication and consequently, a possible influence upon the third level. In addition, his important teaching position at Cambridge would have enabled him to have been in direct contact with the next generation of preachers.

More importantly, Raven's work on pacifism may well have given it a degree of religious and academic legitimation which it previously lacked at the second, third and even fourth levels. At a time in the 1930s when the prospect of war was increasing, it would have been politically expedient to identify all pacifists as either anarchists or cowards. However, with the espousal of the cause by people like Raven, these charges became more difficult. He never hesitated to use his experiences as a chaplain in the First World War to refute the second charge and his chair would ostensibly have refuted the first. Just as Clements argues that religious leaders provided legitimation for the Labour Party in New Zealand,[48] so it is possible to argue that Raven and others provided legitimation for pacifism in Britain during the 1930s, even for those not normally associated with the churches.

Overall, a varied pattern of social significance begins to emerge. Without claiming that theology in any way acts as a 'key' variable within contemporary Britain, a clear possibility arises that it may, at times, be socially significant in shaping attitudes. People outside the churches in the 1930s may never have heard of Raven, let alone actually read his books, but he may nevertheless have made an important contribution to the general legitimation of pacifism at that time.

A very similar argument can be advanced from an analysis of the thoroughgoing pacifist sect, rather than the individual pacifist theologian. Certainly it is possible to maintain, if, for example, one compares contemporary Quakers with contemporary Jehovah's Witnesses, that theological considerations may determine their particular responses to war and that these responses, in turn, may be significant within society as a whole. Without, of course, setting such claims too high—most people within society are not, after all, thoroughgoing pacifists, or even, perhaps, selective pacifists—a serious possibility can be advanced that theology does act at times as an independent variable.

The response of the Jehovah's Witnesses to war provides a particularly startling example of the way specifically theological considerations may be determinative. Strictly speaking, they are not thoroughgoing pacifists, since, if called upon, they will fight for the returning Christ.[49] Nevertheless, in practice, they have proved to be the most determined draft-resisters of all contemporary sectarian Christians. Thus, during the last war, of the three groups, Mennonites, Quakers and Jehovah's Witnesses in the States, it was the last group which was the least willing to participate or even to register in the draft—and as a result, some 5,000 served time in prison.[50] Whilst generally avoiding a self-estimation as pacifists, Jehovah's Witnesses are, in effect, the most radically pacifist sect in the West.

It seems likely that, both their tendency to avoid the label of pacifism and their actual thoroughgoing pacifism, are products of their theological beliefs, particularly those involving an imminent parousia. Although their understanding of the latter has changed somewhat since their prediction, that the kingdom of God would begin in 1914, did not materialise in a visible form, it seems clear, at least, that they still base their faith on an imminent cosmic catastrophe. Bryan Wilson argues that they have come to see 1914 as the beginning of a heavenly and invisible kingdom, in which Christ and some of the 'anointed class' began to reign:

> Not all of the 144,000 have as yet died, however: some remain on earth, and until at least some of these are translated to the heavenly sphere there is an interim, in which the world is increasingly experiencing the activities of Satan. Christ is at work judging the nations, and the basis for this judgement is the attitude of the nations towards the kingdom message and its bearers, that is, Jehovah's Witnesses. Those who have rejected the message and persecuted the messengers are the

goats upon whom judgement will be executed at Armageddon—the great war to come. . . . Millions will die, indeed everyone who opposed Jehovah. Thereafter a new heaven with the 144,000 will appear, and a new earth peopled by others loyal to Jehovah and by the resurrected dead. . . . A further judgement at the end of the millennium will test the good done by those who previously had no chance to hear the message of God.[51]

Wilson suggests that their social involvement is minimal, including persumably their involvement in human wars, 'less because of injunctions to keep separate from the world, than because the good Witness is kept busy at Kingdom Hall and in publicising the movement'.[52] Undoubtedly, their tightly controlled organisation, centering upon a publishing enterprise which enforces doctrinal and practical conformity in its members, is crucial to a sociological understanding of them.[53] Nevertheless, in view of the beliefs just outlined, it is hardly surprising that Jehovah's Witnesses are unwilling to participate in any way in political wars, or even to have this unwillingness depicted in the political/moral terms of pacifism. On this interpretation, their rejection of war stems, not from a moral rejection of warfare as such, but rather from a theological position which makes all political and 'this worldly' realities irrelevant. Given a radical 'interim ethic', in which present human structures are to be destroyed at any minute, participation in human wars would be pointless, just as it was for the first-century Christians.

Such an analysis suggests the clear possibility that, in the case of the Jehovah's Witnesses, theological considerations can act as an independent variable in shaping particular responses to war. In the case of contemporary Quakers this evidence is not so obvious, since other factors in their historical development, notably their comparative acceptance by society at large, may have helped to shape their 'representative' and politically active type of thoroughgoing pacifism.[54] Yet, even with them, it seems possible that their theological understanding of individual conscience did determine this pacifism. Certainly, it would be difficult for a conscientous Quaker, unlike an Anglican or a Roman Catholic, to accept a particular war as 'just' on the evidence of an outside authority—even those few Quakers who have taken part in wars in the past have tended to conform to my third, rather than to my second, ideal type.[55]

It seems possible also, that it is precisely their stress on individual conscience which has made the Quakers' attitude towards war influential upon those who would not otherwise have been sympathetic to pacifists. In the English context, Bainton argues that 'the Quakers by their allegiance to conscience convinced the government of the rights of conscience, and for the first time were accorded exemption from military service on this ground in 1802'.[56] And Wilson, having suggested that their stress since the mid-nineteenth century on charity was an expression of Quaker conscience, maintains that 'their good work as non-combatants in (First World) War earned them the respect of many who did not share their pacifist principles'.[57]

At least two possible ways emerge in which the Quakers' pacifism may have acted as an independent variable within society. By the nineteenth century they had become politically active and have remained so ever since, exercising an apparent influence disproportionate to their numbers. As a result, on the specific issue of war, they have campaigned, not simply for the legal and political recognition of conscientious objectors, but also reconciliation between warfaring nations. It is no accident that Quaker House is set beside the United Nations buildings in New York, to promote informal conversations between visiting diplomats.[58]

Nevertheless, political activity *per se* may not have been the only way in which they have proved influential within society. It seems possible that they provided an important religious and moral legitimation of pacifism. The rejection of human wars by the Jehovah's Witnesses is apparently too interconnected with their radical sectarian beliefs to be entertained seriously by many other than their own members. That of the Quakers, on the other hand, involves (albeit radically) an element with a rather broader appeal, namely, individual conscience. When this appeal is allied to their observable charitable works, its social significance becomes a real possibility.

The sociologist is, I believe, presented here with a strong

possibility that theology, however socially determined in itself, may act at times as an independent variable within society. In the next chapter I shall explore this possibility further, in relation to a single case-study.

5

The Social Significance of the 'Honest to God' Debate

I HAVE argued that there is a possibility that theology, even contemporary theology, may at times be socially significant. That is to say, that its influence may sometimes extend beyond the restricted confines of academic theologians and even beyond the confines of the academic community as a whole. If this possibility is accepted, then a sociological account of theology may have to be taken more seriously than hitherto by sociologists of religion. This chapter is offered in the pursuit of this claim, focusing, as it does, upon a single case-study, in the hope of showing that theological ideas may act as independent variables within society, albeit not always in the way that their authors intend.

The last two decades have witnessed a number of movements within Western Christian theology, some showing considerable interconnections with each other and others appearing mutually exclusive. For instance, these decades have seen a continuing polemic between neo-orthodox types of theology on the one hand and liberal types on the other, some of the former depending heavily upon the persisting influence of Barth and some of the latter upon that of Bultmann. In addition, a number of types of philosophical theology, including process theology, have proved influential, at least within theological circles. Most recently, differing forms of political theology have gained a new resurgence within the West, deriving at least part of their impetus from the Third World. An exhaustive account of all the differing types of theology to be found in the last twenty years would be inappropriate here, although it is relevant to note, in passing, that few indeed are confined to particular denominations. Proponents of most major theological movements would be found in each denomination, whether Protestant or Catholic.

One theological movement which caused an immense impact on both the academic theological world and the ecclesiastical one, was that of 'secular' theology. This label covers an admittedly diffuse body of writing—including, in some understandings, anything from attempts to 'demythologise' the Gospel, through attempts to respond to a presumed process of secularisation, to the most thoroughgoing 'Death of God' theologies—but, for convenience, it refers to those radical theologians who during the 1960s reflected critically upon Christian belief. Indeed, it was both their concentration upon belief, rather than upon the 'sequelae' of belief (as in political theology) or upon the antecedents of belief (as in philosophical theology), and their radical treatment of this belief (not of course confined to them or to the 1960s) which bound them together as an identifiable theological movement.

Their impact upon the theological and ecclesiastical worlds—if this is measured in terms of the amount of literature and debate that they have engendered—has been greater than that of any other theological movement during these two decades. Whatever the theological merits of 'secular' theology, which are obviously not relevant here, the movement may be of real interest to the sociologist of knowledge. It presents the latter with the possibility of observing how socially constructed knowledge can yet be socially significant.

Within this chapter, I intend to concentrate upon the *Honest to God* debate, itself an important element within the 'secular' theology movement. Elsewhere I have attempted to analyse the societal assumptions of some of the theologians who took part in this debate.[1] Here I will focus instead upon their and others' response to *Honest to God* itself. Such focus will, I believe, help to clarify the social role of theological factors more clearly than would a more generalised analysis of 'secular' theology. Undoubtedly, the response to *Honest to God* cannot be understood fully apart from the latter, but it can, at least, present the sociologist with an empirically manageable subject.

A Priori Justification:
Even a preliminary reading of *Honest to God* and the debate that it provoked amongst theologians, will suggest to the

sociologist a number of social determinants. Indeed, it was a key argument of one of Robinson's most strident critics that he, together with Paul van Buren and John Knox, was part and parcel of the secularisation process. Thus, as I have argued before,[2] E. L. Mascall locates Robinson in the Protestant school which 'takes as its starting-point the outlook of contemporary secularised man and demands that the traditional faith of Christendom should be completely transformed in order to conform to it'.[3] In effect, Mascall argues, we are forced to 'de-supernaturalise' Christianity simply because the world can no longer accept the 'supernatural': the Gospel is compelled to conform to the world and not the world to the Gospel. Mascall evidently believes this to be a total misunderstanding of the role of theology and in his judgement Robinson 'completely capitulates to the outlook of the contemporary world'.[4] Mascall would apparently find no difficulties in the claim of the sociologist of knowledge that *Honest to God* is a socially constructed reality and a manifest product of its social context.

One need accept neither Mascall's implicit theory of secularisation nor his particular theological critique of Robinson, in order to agree with a part of his analysis. Precisely because Robinson was so concerned in *Honest to God* to write in the light of contemporary plausibility structures as he understood them, he was at the same time clearly susceptible to being determined by them. An analysis of the book in terms of the sociology of knowledge might anticipate that it, more than most theological works, displayed clear signs of being socially determined. On this understanding social relevance and social determination are closely correlated.

On the other hand, Mascall's critique of *Honest to God* also provides evidence for its possible significance. Clearly, he thought that it, Paul van Buren's *The Secular Meaning of the Gospel*[5] and John Knox's *The Church and the Reality of Christ*[6] were sufficiently important to warrant a complete book devoted to attacking them. In his Preface he even refers to them as 'outstanding expressions of a radical and destructive attitude to traditional Christianity which has obtained a foothold in many academic circles in the United States and the United Kingdom, though until the publication of *Honest to God* it was little known

85

to the general public and to the majority of the parochial clergy'.[7] It is true that Mascall already had a reputation for producing refutations of contemporary theological works. Thus, in 1962, he wrote a detailed critique, entitled *Up and Down in Adria*,[8] of the Cambridge symposium *Soundings*:[9] and in 1963 he produced a booklet, *Theology and Images*,[10] largely concerned with refuting A. C. Bridge's *Images of God*.[11] Nevertheless, it is evident that he did believe that *Honest to God* had proved influential beyond the confines of academic theology.

It is precisely the trauma that *Honest to God* created in the theological and ecclesiastical worlds that provides the main *prima facie* evidence for its social significance. Robinson himself claimed subsequently that he had never anticipated this trauma:

> The publicity-explosion was neither sought nor expected. If there had been a desire to exploit the market, (a) I should not have given the manuscript to a religious publisher, (b) there would have been a special publicity-campaign to launch it, and (c) I should have written a very different book.[12]

However, a week before publication he did contribute an article to the *Observer*, which the editorial entitled 'Our Image of God Must Go'. Certainly, he argued that he wrote this, not to cause publicity for the book, but rather because it provided him with 'a real opportunity outside the normal channels of the Church to engage at a serious level as a Christian in the intellectual debate of our day'.[13] Nevertheless, this overall argument ignores four non-theological features of *Honest to God*, to which I shall return presently and which may help to explain why the book proved so traumatic and possibly so influential.

For whatever reasons *Honest to God* was written (and possibly Robinson himself when he wrote it did not consider too deeply what its effects might be or even for whom he was writing), its immediate repercussions on the theological and ecclesiastical worlds were immense. The then Archbishop of Canterbury, Michael Ramsey, swiftly published a pamphlet, *Images Old and New*,[14] seeking 'to spread reassurance' as Alasdair MacIntyre suggested at the time,[15] and in effect correcting Robinson's doctrinal position, In his Holland Lectures at Oxford in the following year, Ramsey continued on the same theme, but

without specifically mentioning *Honest to God*.[16] By 1969 he
could write:

> Since the stirring of the theological waters some five years ago
> by Bishop John Robinson's *Honest to God*, theology in England
> has to a large extent lost what we can now see to have been a
> long-established insularity. It was perhaps that insularity which
> made some of us slow to grasp what was happening. It was not
> that some people called 'new theologians' were inventing
> theologies of compromise with the secular world: it was rather
> that they were trying to meet, often in clumsy and muddled
> ways, pressures and currents already moving powerfully in and
> beyond Christendom.[17]

The trauma created by *Honest to God* was immediate and
widespread. As a result, it created unprecedented behaviour
amongst religious publishers. Within weeks of its publication,
the Religious Education Press produced O. Fielding Clarke's
For Christ's Sake, seeking to refute 'Dr Robinson's errors and
re-state the Faith in outline'.[18] Clarke himself took time off
from his parish and wrote this fierce chapter-by-chapter
critique of *Honest to God* in only four weeks. The Student Christian Movement Press, which published the book on 19 March
1963, managed to bring out a 283-page response entitled *The
Honest to God Debate* before the end of the same year. This contained a number of fresh articles concerned with the issues
raised by *Honest to God*, 50 letters written to Robinson after its
publication and 23 of its many reviews. Indeed theological
journals throughout the world reviewed the book. Finally the
SCM Press produced a number of subsequent defences by
Robinson of his Christian 'orthodoxy', notably his *The New
Reformation* in 1965 and *Exploration into God* in 1967—quite
apart from a stream of books by other theologians published by
them and other publishers defending and criticising *Honest to
God*.[19] By the end of the 1960s references to the book appear
comparatively seldom, but for a year or two few theological
writers passed it unnoticed. Seldom has there been a comparable trauma in the theological world.

In addition to this trauma, there appeared to be a similar
trauma within the non-theological world arising from *Honest to
God*. Indeed, the fact that it created interest and debate in the

latter world provides further *a priori* justification for the claim that it was socially significant. Michael Ramsey publicly criticised Robinson on television[20]—an unusual step for an Anglican archbishop to take concerning one of his own bishops. T. E. Utley asked the question, 'what should happen to an Anglican bishop who does not believe in God?', in the *Sunday Telegraph*.[21] C. S. Lewis, E. L. Mascall, A. G. N. Flew, Sir Julian Huxley, Edward Carpenter and T. R. Milford all contributed articles on the book to the *Observer*.[22] Bryan Green wrote for the *Birmingham Post*, R. P. C. Hanson for the *Irish Times*, Rudolf Bultmann for *Die Zeit* and C. F. Evans spoke on the radio.[23] Rarely can there have been so many academic theologians, senior ecclesiastics and others debating about a single book—least of all on the mass media. Writing only months after the publication of *Honest to God*, David Edwards observed:

> The book appears to have sold more quickly than any new book of serious theology in the history of the world. Already over 350,000 copies are in print in Britain, America and Australia, and it is also being published in German, French, Swedish, Dutch, Danish, Italian and Japanese. The discussion has spread even more widely than the readership. Television programmes and sound radio broadcasts, cartoons and satirical jokes, newspaper excerpts and reviews, sermons and Letters to the Editor, swelled the volume of the debate.[24]

The fact that *Honest to God*, unlike most theological or religious works, became a 'best-seller' and that it stimulated over one thousand people to write to Robinson, again indicates that it may have been socially significant. The letters, some of which were reproduced in *The Honest to God Debate* and all of which are being subjected to content-analysis at Leeds University, provide a rich, even if somewhat partisan, source of evidence about the effect of the book on the non-theological public (just as the 27,000 letters evoked by Archbishop Donald Coggan's 'Call to the Nation' are already providing an indication, albeit partisan, of this public).[25] Further, unless the majority of the copies of the book were bought and unread, the fact that so many were sold is a strong indication that its influence extended far beyond the circles of academic theology.

One final piece of evidence should be mentioned. Apart from

his initial article in the *Observer*, Robinson, as a direct result of the trauma created by *Honest to God*, was invited to contribute to a variety of 'popular' newspapers and journals. Thus, he wrote articles for the *Sunday Mirror*, the *Sun*, *TV Times* and *Tit-Bits*. It seems likely that he may have reached an audience here which is seldom influenced directly by academic theologians.

Taken together, these various strands of evidence—most of them unique to *Honest to God*—appear to present strong *prima facie* evidence for the social significance of the work. Of course, there is also strong evidence (even if one is not a sociologist of knowledge methodologically committed to viewing all ideas as socially constructed) to suggest that it is socially conditioned. Nevertheless, however much influenced by society, *Honest to God* would seem, in turn, to have been an influence upon society. If ever there was an instance of a theological work having an effect upon a non-theological public, this would appear to be it. There does, indeed, seem to be *a priori* justification for the claim that the book acted as an independent variable.

The Paradox of Honest to God:
None the less, *Honest to God* also creates a paradox. A content analysis of the book suggests features which appear too technical for a non-theological readership and even some of the central ideas within it are not elaborated clearly and succinctly. Robinson's often-repeated claim that he did not intend it to be a 'best-seller', reaching such a wide audience, would seem correct. Certainly, if *Honest to God* is compared stylistically with some of his more 'popular' writings clear differences emerge.[26] It is worth outlining briefly its main contents.

The contents of *Honest to God* fall naturally under four headings—God, Christ, Prayer and Morality. Three chapters are devoted to the first topic and just one each to the other three. The final chapter, 'Recasting the Mould', repeats some of Robinson's themes, but it too is largely concerned with images of God. It is hardly surprising, then, that much of the subsequent debate amongst theologians centred upon theistic images and models. Curiously, though, it is precisely this feature of the book which may have proved most difficult for non-theological readers. Such concepts as '*deus ex machina*', 'demythologising', 'existentialism' and 'being' are used without explanation. In addition, he makes frequent reference to Tillich, Bultmann and Bonhoeffer in a manner more designed for theologians than for the general public.

Robinson starts by suggesting that there has been a 're-luctant revolution' in our thinking about God, since, 'in place of a God who is literally or physically "up there" we have accepted, as part of our mental furniture, a God who is spiritually or metaphysically "out there"'.[27] In this respect we are different from our fore-fathers, even though 'every one of us lives with some mental picture of a God "out there", a God who "exists" above and beyond the world, a God "to" whom we pray and to whom we "go" when we die'.[28] He argues that these spatial terms are now an 'offence' to many, though he fully realises that 'to be asked to give up any idea of a Being "out there" at all will appear to be an outright denial of God'.[29] Nevertheless, he maintains that we are being asked to do just this.

Like Tillich, Robinson believes that traditional proofs for the existence of God are irrelevant, since their result would be merely 'a further piece of existence, that might conceivably not have been there'.[30] So in the second chapter, he argues:

> We must start the other way round. God is, by definition, ultimate reality. And one cannot argue whether ultimate reality *exists*. One can only ask what ultimate reality is like— whether, for instance, in the last analysis what lies at the heart of things and governs their working is to be described in personal or impersonal categories.[31]

Thus, with Tillich, he prefers to talk about God as 'Being' rather than 'a Being', seeing parallels in Bultmann's programme of 'demythologising' and Bonhoeffer's castigations of the 'God of religion'. He is aware that this demolition of traditional theism will 'appear to leave many people bereft and "without God in the world"'[32] and attract a charge of atheism to himself, but he still believes it to be necessary in the interests of 'intelligent faith'.

One of the surprising features of *Honest to God* is that the first forty-four pages are almost wholly negative and icono-clastic. In them Robinson criticises a series of traditional images of God and only then does he offer alternative ones. It is possible that this is one of the features that contributed to its overall impact. Certainly, it is not until the third chapter that he opts unequivocally for Tillich's image of God as 'The Ground of Our Being', arguing that the model of 'depth' is preferable to that of 'height':

> There is no doubt that this simple substitution can make much religious language suddenly appear more relevant. For we are familiar today with depth psychology, and with the idea that ultimate truth is deep and profound. Moreover, while 'spiritual wickedness in high places', and all the mythology of angelic powers which the Biblical writers associate with it, seems to the modern man a fantastic phantasmagoria, similar, equally mythological, language when used by Freud of conflicts in the unconscious appears perfectly acceptable.[33]

Using the concept of 'depth' as his starting-point, Robinson claims, with Tillich, that God is 'the infinite and inexhaustible depth and ground of all being, of our ultimate concern, of what we take seriously without reservation'.[34] Aware that this claim could be mistaken for a Feuerbachian transformation of theology into anthropology, he insists that 'theological statements are indeed affirmations about human existence—but they are affirmations about the ultimate ground and depth of that existence'.[35] Distinguishing this position further from naturalism, he maintains that 'the necessity for the name "God" lies in the fact that our being has depths which naturalism, whether evolutionary, mechanistic, dialectical or humanistic, cannot or will not recognise'.[36]

By comparison with the first three chapters, the fourth, on Christ, received little attention from the critics. In structure, though, it is similar to the section on God, since it seeks to disclaim traditional theological images, before offering a Tillichian alternative. Thus, it opens with a characteristically stylised account:

> Traditional Christology has worked with a frankly supranaturalist scheme. Popular religion has expressed this mythologically, professional theology metaphysically. For this way of thinking, the Incarnation means that God the Son came down to earth, and was born, lived and died within this world as a man. From

'out there' there graciously entered into the human scene one who was not 'of it' and yet who lived genuinely and completely within it.[37]

Robinson maintains that this traditional interpretation of christology almost inevitably suggests that 'Jesus was not a man born and bred . . . he looked like a man, he talked like a man, but underneath he was God dressed up—like Father Christmas'.[38] Here too it is evident that *Honest to God* presents the reader with an unusual mixture of technical theological terms, idiomatic epithets and caricature.

Moving from this negative beginning and having already rejected a purely naturalist interpretation of christology, Robinson suggests, with echoes of D. M. Baillie,[39] that Jesus 'reveals God by being utterly transparent to him'.[40] With echoes of Tillich, he continues:

> It is in Jesus, and Jesus alone, that there is nothing of self to be seen, but solely the ultimate, unconditional love of God . . . it is as he empties himself not of his Godhead but of himself, of any desire to focus attention on himself, of any craving to be 'on an equality with God', that he reveals God. For it is in making himself nothing, in his utter self-surrender to others in love, that he discloses and lays bare the Ground of man's being as Love.[41]

This combination of elements from Baillie and Tillich, in a reversal of the kenotic theory in christology, is arguably one of the more original features of *Honest to God*. Yet, it received comparatively little attention from the theologians.

The fifth chapter is concerned with prayer and worship, areas in which his views were already well known amongst theologians.[42] Following his characteristic procedure, he starts with a critical observation:

> Liturgy and worship would, on the face of it, seem to be concerned essentially with what takes place in a consecrated building, with the holy rather than the common, with 'religion' rather than 'life'. They belong to, and indeed virtually constitute, that area or department of experience which appeals to 'the religious type', to those who 'like that sort of thing' or 'get something out of it'.[43]

Too often, he maintains, communion becomes individualistic devotion in which we 'make our communion' with 'the God out there'. He argues that instead communion is essentially a communal event: the function of worship is 'to focus, sharpen and deepen our response to the world and to other people beyond the point of proximate concern (of liking, self-interest, limited commitment, etc.) to that of ultimate concern; to purify and correct our loves in the light of Christ's love; and in him to find the grace and power to be the reconciled and reconciling community'.[44]

On private prayer, he is scathing about a type of 'monastic spirituality' which conceives it as a 'turning aside from the business of "the world" to "be with God"'.[45] It should be seen rather as a 'penetration through the world to God'.[46] Again, in typically Tillichian terms, he concludes that 'to pray for another is to expose both oneself and him to the common ground of our being; it is to see one's concern for him in terms of *ultimate* concern, to let *God* into the relationship'.[47]

The final theme that he considers is that of morality, arguing that 'it is impossible to reassess one's doctrine of God, of how one understands the transcendent, without bringing one's view of morality into the same melting-pot'.[48] There is, however, a crucial difference between this area and that of doctrine; here there has already been, he believes, a revolution in public opinion. Consequently, 'our only task is to relate it correctly to the previous revolution we have described and to try to discern what should be the Christian attitude to it'.[49] Nevertheless, Robinson still adheres to his method of critical caricature followed by Tillichian alternatives. Thus, in response to this revolution in morals, he claims:

> There are plenty of voices within the Church greeting it with vociferous dismay. The religious sanctions are losing their strength, the moral landmarks are disappearing beneath the flood, the nation is in danger. This is the end-term of the apostasy from Christianity: the fathers rejected the doctrine, the children have abandoned the morals . . . Christianity is identified *tout court* with the old, traditional morality.[50]

Such normative approaches to morality, he believes, distort the teaching of Jesus. The latter 'is saying that love, utterly unconditional love, admits of no accommodation; you cannot define in advance situations in which it can be satisfied with less than complete and unreserved self-giving.'[51] This account of morality in terms of 'situation ethics' is then transcribed into Tillichian terms:

> In ethics this means accepting as the basis of moral judgements the actual concrete relationship in all its particularity, refusing to subordinate it to any universal norm or to treat it merely as a case, but yet, in the depth of that unique relationship, meeting and responding to the claims of the sacred, the holy and the absolutely unconditional. For the Christian it means recognising as the ultimate ground of our being which is thus encountered, and as the basis of every relationship and every decision, the unconditional love of Jesus Christ, 'the man for others'. [52]

Writing at a time when Fletcher's 'situation ethics' was still relatively unknown in Britain, Robinson's views on morality caused considerable debate amongst theologians and a number of books discussed the 'new morality' (as he called it).[53] Before long, however, this attention was deflected to Fletcher himself, with the publication of *Situation Ethics*.[54] But, for a while, the impact of this chapter was almost as great as that of the first three chapters—at least amongst theologians and preachers.

In his final chapter he admits that 'it will doubtless seem to some that I have by implication abandoned the Christian faith and practice altogether'.[55] However, he maintains that the changes are essential and that they leave 'the fundamental truth of the Gospel unaffected':[56]

> I believe that *unless* we are prepared for the kind of revolution of which I have spoken it *will come* to be abandoned. And that will be because it is moulded, in the form we know it, by a cast of thought that belongs to a past age—the cast of thought which, with their different emphases, Bultmann describes as 'mythological', Tillich as 'supranaturalist', and Bonhoeffer as 'religious'.[57]

We must be prepared, he maintains, to let everything 'go into the melting', even 'our most cherished religious categories and moral absolutes' and certainly 'our image of God himself'.[58]

Even this bare summary of the contents of *Honest to God* creates a paradox, which most contemporary commentators

94

found almost impossible to explain. The book relies heavily on established theologians (notably Tillich, who is used at every constructive point) and it uses many unexplained technical theological terms from them and others—yet it became a 'best seller'. It may, indeed, be doubted whether more than a small minority of those who bought *Honest to God* were sufficiently equipped to cope with its stylistic and conceptual difficulties. Whereas it is quite possible to believe that it caused an impact amongst those specifically trained in theology (who may not all have been thoroughly familiar with Tillich or Fletcher), its impact on the non-theological world is more perplexing.

The sociologist, then, is faced with a paradox. Whilst he might accept that *Honest to God* was socially significant amongst those with theological training, he may well find it difficult to maintain that it had a similar cognitive effect on those without this training. Even the *a priori* justification already advanced of the generalised social significance of the work does not actually dissolve this difficulty; rather it serves to heighten it. The two sets of evidence—one suggesting that *Honest to God* made an impact well beyond normal theological circles and the other suggesting that stylistically and conceptually it would have been incomprehensible outside these circles—appear mutually contradictory.

In the face of this apparent paradox it becomes imperative to subject the impact of *Honest to God* to rigorous analysis. More specifically, it is important to assess its social significance in terms of the four levels of analysis which I suggested earlier—namely, theologians, preachers, listeners and outsiders.

Four Levels of Social Significance:
In the light of all the preceding evidence, there can be little doubt that *Honest to God* was socially significant amongst both theologians and those academics with an interest in theology. Naturally many were highly critical of the work, not a few calling into question Robinson's status as a Christian and as a 'theist'—the most famous claiming that 'what is striking about Dr. Robinson's book is first and foremost that he is an atheist'[59]—but few failed to respond to it in some way. Whatever they thought of its academic merits, most responded to

the generalised interest in it by reviewing, commenting upon, or simply referring to it *en passant*. Few theological works can have received such intense inspection within the theological world, although many can claim a more enduring inspection.

As already indicated, two elements in *Honest to God* received particular attention from theologians. The first and by far the most prominent, was its concern with images of God: the second was its concern with morality. The latter soon developed into an argument about the merits or demerits of 'situation ethics' and consequently tended to focus instead upon Fletcher, but the former continued to centre upon Robinson for some years, not fading until the end of the decade.

Initially, the theological debate about images of God concentrated upon the cognitive issue of whether or not the Tillichian language proposed by Robinson could adequately represent Christian belief. Paul van Buren's *The Secular Meaning of the Gospel*, published very shortly after *Honest to God* and owing nothing directly to it, stimulated this debate still further, since here was an attempt to translate the Gospel into thoroughly 'secular' terms. Robinson did not wholly accept this radical translation of theistic language into language about 'contagious freedom', but he did welcome it as 'a major contribution' to the debate.[60] Taken together, these two books in particular, stimulated a series of other books, attempting to isolate the key issues of belief involved in the debate.[61]

Before long, however, another issue became dominant in the theological response to *Honest to God*, namely, a focus upon the issue of secularisation. As I have tried to show elsewhere, although the term 'secularisation' appears very seldom in *Honest to God* itself, it was used by Robinson quite frequently in the subsequent debate and became a central issue alike amongst his critics and defenders.[62] Clearly, his initial argument depended on (a) the belief that there was a process of secularisation (or something very much like it) apparent within the West and (b) that Christians should respond positively to it. Whilst few at the time questioned (a), many, like Mascall,[63] were thoroughly opposed to (b).

This first level of analysis presents the fewest problems for the sociologist. Given my definition of theology as essentially a written discipline, he has only to refer back to the literature of the 1960s in order to assess the social significance of *Honest to God* amongst theologians. It should be made clear, of course, that the term 'theologians', in accordance with this definition, includes many churchmen, in addition to academics who chose to write on the themes raised by the book. Overall, it would appear that it did have an immense effect upon contemporary theology within Britain and indeed upon theology within much of the Western world. Few other works of theology can have achieved such an immediate effect.

Analysis of the social significance of *Honest to God* at the other three levels is not so straightforward. Here, the sociologist can no longer rely so directly on written records, but must, instead, search for other indicators. In addition, he must take account of the paradox already outlined.

Since many preachers have received a theological training, it can be assumed that they read *Honest to God* with more understanding than those without such training. At the least, they could have been familiar with some of the unexplained technical theological terms used in the book. Certainly, there are indications that they responded to some of the cognitive issues raised by Robinson and particularly those concerned with images of God. Few who worked as ministers at the time can have failed to notice the widespread anxiety expressed by their colleagues over these issues. Bryan Wilson depicted this well when he wrote in 1966:

> The scepticism of modern society has affected the clerical profession profoundly. The attempt to find other levels at which religious propositions are true—that is to say, levels other than the common-sense and literal level—has led to widely diverse clerical interpretations of religion in its contemporary meaning. Clerics have now come to disbelieve in the ultimacy of any answers which they can supply about social questions, as they did earlier about physical questions. As the range of empirical information has increased, acquisition of the knowledge of it and the skills to analyse it and interpret it pass beyond the range of clerical education. The awareness of the relativity of modern knowledge has made the cleric more guarded and less confident in the intellectual content of religion.[64]

This passage bristles with assumptions that a number of subsequent sociologists have found difficult to accept. Thus, it assumes that 'modern society' is indeed sceptical and it is set within the overall context of Wilson's thoroughgoing secularisation model.[65] Further, Wilson clearly believes that one can distinguish between 'common-sense' or 'literal' levels at which religious propositions may be true and 'other' such levels—despite the theological truism that no human language can be applied to God univocally.[66] Finally, he proceeds to corroborate this analysis of the clergy not only with statistics largely drawn from the Church of England, showing a decline in the overall number of priests, a decline in ordinands, a decline of graduates in proportion to non-graduates, a decline in their remuneration by the Church and an overall increase in their average age, but also with his theory that ecumenism is increasingly acting as the 'new faith' of the clergy in the absence of theistic beliefs, in an age 'when traditional ideas about God have been radically challenged by bishops of the Church.'[67] Again, subsequent analysis has not always confirmed his claims. So, it is possible that his statistically based analysis tends to ignore less religious variables (such as inflation)[68] and that his understanding of ecumenism is sociologically incomplete.[69]

Nevertheless, as a depiction of *the clergy* in the mid-1960s Bryan Wilson's account may not be too inaccurate. In retrospect, this time proved to be a fairly traumatic one for a number of clergy, as some of the letters from them to Robinson indicated.[70] Cognitive as well as functional, dilemmas did seem to play a part and it is likely that *Honest to God* was a significant variable within this situation. Certainly, David Edwards, writing shortly after the book's publication, believed that 'many printed comments, and reports of sermons and addresses, emphasised the distress of many Christian believers'.[71] Although a number of radical theological works could have caused this effect amongst the clergy (who presumably had access to books other than *Honest to God*) the very success and wide availability of the latter makes it an obvious candidate as a key factor within this situation. Certainly, Paul van Buren's *The Secular Meaning of the Gospel* presented the non-academic with semantic difficulties, owing to its frequent use of contemporary philosophy, which, comparatively speaking, *Honest to God* did not.

If this analysis is correct and the cognitive issues raised by *Honest to God* and debated at length by other theologians really did impinge, in part at least, upon the preachers, then it seems possible that they may also have engaged the 'listeners'—a group that includes both those who actually read the book and/or writings about it and those who simply heard the preachers. Of course, there has been evidence for some time suggesting that congregations may be theologically confused.[72] Exploiting this evidence Alasdair MacIntyre ruefully claimed that 'the creed of the English is that there is no God and that it is wise to pray to him from time to time'.[73] More seriously, even David Martin, despite his dismissal of the secularisation model, argues that 'the religion of modern Britain is a deistic, moralistic religion-in-general, which combines a fairly high practice of personal prayer with a considerable degree of superstition'.[74] As a result, it would take an ingenious survey to show that this cognitive confusion amongst the listeners was either heightened or diminished by *Honest to God*. The possibility, nevertheless, that it might have had some effect at this level cannot thereby be overruled.

Nevertheless, the paradox outlined earlier remains. *Honest to God* sold widely amongst a non-theological public, but it must have been, at least partially, incomprehensible to it. Even the fact that Robinson contributed a number of far simpler articles to 'popular' magazines and newspapers does not resolve this paradox, since it was the book itself that sold so widely. Any sociological consideration of the social significance of *Honest to God* must take this paradox into account.

It is possible, though, that my analysis up to this point has been too cognitive-oriented. It is too easy for the sociologist of knowledge to assume that it is ideas, as ideas, which are socially significant and not ideas as they are in fact presented to the listener. Once analysis focuses upon the latter, four non-theological features of *Honest to God*, require particular attention. Together, they may help to explain both why the book became a 'best-seller' and what its generalised impact may have been.

The first feature to be isolated is that in *Honest to God* Robinson stressed his function as a bishop. So, 'it belongs to the office of a bishop . . .' are the opening words of the preface.[75] In the first chapter he claims that 'as a bishop I could happily get on with most of my work without ever being forced to discuss such questions':[76] at the end of the chapter he writes that he is 'deliberately writing as an ordinary churchman', not as a professional theologian.[77] From the perspective of publicity, the fact that the writer of the book was a bishop was crucial: all clergy are vulnerable to publicity and bishops even more so. At the same time that Robinson was writing, Bishop Pike was causing an immense stir in the States and soon afterwards the British newspapers were reporting that the Bishop of Munich was suspected of war crimes, the Bishop of Southwell had apparently eloped, the Bishop of Leicester had signed a 'keep the cricket tour' petition in the face of anti-apartheid protests and the Bishop of Coventry had condemned pornography. Thus, by stressing his function as a bishop, whilst at the same time writing radical theology, Robinson may well have contributed significantly to its general publicity.

By implication, Wilson would appear to support this suggestion:

> That some clergy themselves become sceptical, and cease to believe in many of the things which laymen believe in as essentials of the faith, or believe in them in an entirely different way, can only be a source of confusion and despair to those who want to believe in certain, and usually simple, truths. A Bishop Barnes of Birmingham in the 1930s and 40s, a Bishop Pike of California, and a Bishop Robinson of Woolwich, in the 1960s, are only sources of bewilderment to ordinary believers, some of whom are impious enough to wonder why, if men think as they do, they continue to take their stipends from Churches which commit them, in honesty, to rather different beliefs.[78]

It is interesting to note here that it is the bishops whom Wilson singles out as being socially significant agents of change amongst laypeople.

Secondly, on more than one occasion in *Honest to God*, Robinson suggests that what he is writing would be regarded by many as 'heretical'. The labels 'heretic' and 'atheist' occur in several parts of the book. So, at the end of the preface he writes that 'what I have tried to say, in a tentative and exploratory way, may seem to be radical, and doubtless to many heretical'.[79] In the section on God, he admits that what he has to say on the subject will be 'resisted as a denial of the Gospel' by 90 per cent of the people:[80] in the section on morality, he claims that his views are not 'what men expect the Church to stand for' and that they will be regarded 'as profoundly shocking':[81] and, in the final chapter, he states that some will think he has 'abandoned the Christian faith and practice altogether'.[82] The general effect of hinting so often that he may be a 'heretic' or even an 'atheist' is to make the book highly provocative. Certainly, a number of people responded by agreeing with these labels as a correct depiction of him.[83]

Thirdly, *Honest to God* is thoroughly iconoclastic. It has already been shown that each of the four sections—on God, Christ, Prayer and Morality—begins with a demolition of traditional images. In particular, the first of these, in which Robinson seeks to discredit traditional images of God as he understands them, extends to page forty-four. Even if the specific issues which he is discussing are unclear to the non-theological reader, the fact that he is attempting to break down existing beliefs is perfectly clear.

Fourthly, *Honest to God*, as a work in theology, contains a surprising amount of caricature. As I have indicated, his characteristic style in each of the sections is to demolish traditional images in a stylised and caricatured form and only then to offer a Tillichian alternative. Thus, writing in the first section on God, he suggests that for most Christians and non-Christians 'he has been more of a Grandfather in heaven, a kindly Old Man who could be pushed into one corner':[84] in the second, he compares the traditional Christ to an 'astronaut': in the third, traditional prayers are termed 'spiritual refills': and in the fourth, traditional morality is said to 'come straight from heaven'. Part of the protest from traditional theologians was, in fact, that their position had been distorted and caricatured.[85]

It seems likely that these four features taken together—an emphasis on episcopacy, a suggestion of 'heresy', of iconoclasm

101

and of caricature—served to give *Honest to God* its distinctively polemical and provocative character. Given that the cognitive issues involved in the book would have been blurred for the reader without a theological training by Robinson's frequent use of technical theological terms, it may have been these features which proved socially significant at this level.

This suggestion receives a certain degree of confirmation from a comparison of *Honest to God* with Robinson's two subsequent works, *The New Reformation?* and *Exploration into God*. Both of these books are distinctly more eirenic than the first and, although they continue to deal with the same substantive issues, they no longer contain the four features to the same extent. So, in *The New Reformation?* Robinson rarely mentions his function as a bishop and no longer suggests that his position will be regarded as 'heretical' or 'atheistic'. Even the opening chapter, with its seemingly iconoclastic title, 'Troubling of the Waters', proves to be eirenic and his concept of 'reformation' turns out to be 'marked as much by evolution as by revolution'.[86] The caricatures of traditional images are also less evident in this later book. In *Exploration into God*, Robinson appears even more keen to avoid provocation, arguing now that in *Honest to God* 'I was *taking for granted* most of what I believed',[87] and offering an acount of the transcendence of God. Even the chapter titles become eirenic; so, instead of a chapter entitled 'The End of Theism?', as in *Honest to God*, the later book has a chapter entitled 'The Displacement Effect of Theism'. In the following chapter on the 'Death of God' theology, Robinson is far more critical of Paul van Buren's *The Secular Meaning of the Gospel* than he ever was in *The Honest to God Debate*. Significantly, neither of these later books, with their absence of the polemical features of *Honest to God*, became 'best sellers'.

It is possible that these four features also had a certain effect on the fourth level, that of the 'outsiders' (i.e. those who neither read any parts of the debate nor heard preachers at the time). Whilst it cannot credibly be claimed that everybody in Britain would have heard of John Robinson or *Honest to God*, or would have pondered deeply the substantive issues he was raising, it might be supposed that there was some awareness in the public at large that a bishop had been saying provocative things about matters usually accepted by Christians. Certainly, the efforts of Robinson himself to communicate in 'popular' magazines and newspapers[88] might have served to increase this awareness. It is more doubtful, though, whether the general public would have given much consideration (as Wilson suggests) to the discrepancy of beliefs between the clergy and the laity.

Finally, the possibility cannot be ignored that *Honest to God* may have played a part in legitimating existing religious doubt in any of the four levels. It is apparent from some of the letters sent to Robinson after publication, that people, in varying positions and with varying degrees of theological sophistication, felt relief that a bishop had openly expressed doubts on matters of doctrinal orthodoxy.[89] Others, of course, expressed hostility to this expression of doubts, but amongst those who expressed relief (and there is no means of knowing how widespread this reaction was) the book appeared to be an important legitimating factor. Here again, then, the possibility is raised that theology may act at times as a legitimating influence within society.[90]

The phenomenon of *Honest to God* and the debate that it provoked, presents the sociologist of knowledge with an exceptionally important case-study. It seems clear that the book was socially significant amongst both theologians and preachers in the mid-1960s. In addition, it seems likely that it was socially significant amongst congregations and amongst those acquainted with religious literature at the time. It may even have been socially significant amongst the general public. Its influence varied in content from one group to another, but it would appear to have been widespread. If nothing else, this case-study indicates that theology, however determined by society, may in turn act as an independent variable within it.

6

Variables Within Applied Theology

THE PREVIOUS chapters have attempted to provide an account
of theology in terms of the sociology of knowledge. Theology
has been interpreted first as a dependent social variable and
then as an independent social variable. The next chapter will
suggest how these two interpretations can be correlated into a
single interactionist analysis of the discipline. Thus, the
overall task of the book has been dictated by the canons of the
sociology of knowledge.

However, the present chapter represents a digression from
this overall task, since it will be concerned exclusively with
the needs of the theologian. More specifically, it will maintain
that the methods outlined in the previous chapters for analysing
theology can be adopted directly within 'applied theology'. It
will be argued that, too often, sociology is treated, at best, by
the theologian as an ancillary discipline, affecting theology
only in its more marginal aspects. In contrast, given a shift
away from prescriptive and towards descriptive understandings
of 'applied theology', sociology may assume a position of great
importance—no longer peripheral, but actually integral, to
theology.

This is a major claim that will be resisted by a number of
theologians. But, it should be stressed at the outset that the
sociologist *qua* sociologist cannot dictate to the theologian
what should be the nature of his discipline. He cannot insist on
a particular understanding of either Christian ethics or practical
theology simply because it accords with his particular socio-
theological correlation. That would indeed be to commit a
category error.[1] All that he can maintain, as a sociologist, is
that, *given* a particular understanding of 'applied theology',
then such a correlation is possible.

105

Because of the lack of theoretical clarity in much of the 'applied theology' literature, it will be necessary to start with an account of prescriptive and descriptive approaches within it. However, no claim will be made that sociology can supply a complete account of applied theology, or that the latter can be reduced without remainder to the former. Most accounts of Christian ethics or practical theology as descriptive, rather than prescriptive, disciplines include a critical element. They are not content simply to describe: they do wish to distinguish between more and less adequate understandings of theological or ethical concepts. Thus, although their central focus is not upon it, they do contain a prescriptive element. It assumes a secondary role without being entirely absent.

Prescriptive Understandings of Applied Theology:
In Christian ethics and practical theology, the common feature requiring the label 'prescriptive' is that each discipline is viewed essentially as a means of producing tangible solutions to particular problems. Each is seen as the producer of specifiable prescriptions. In Christian ethics, this has taken the form of a widespread emphasis upon decision-making as the principal object of the discipline. The theologian engaged in Christian ethics is attempting to resolve particular ethical dilemmas, albeit from a Christian perspective. In practical (or 'pastoral'—the terms are used synonymously) theology since Schleiermacher, the prescriptive emphasis has taken the form of a general assumption that the discipline is basically concerned with the 'application' of systematic theology, with the provision of prescriptions for the churches or ordinands elaborating how they should act. Frequently this has meant that practical theology is viewed merely as the 'practical' side of theology.

(a) *Prescriptive Practical Theology*: Karl Barth expressed this understanding of practical theology very clearly, when he suggested that 'practical theology is, as the name implies, theology in transition to the practical work of the community— to proclamation'.[2] For him:

> The question of practical theology is how the Word of God may be served by human words. How can this Word, which has been

received in the testimony of the Bible and of Church history and has been considered in its contemporary self-preservation, be served also through the community for the benefit of the world that surrounds it? . . . The real question is the problem of the language which must be employed by those who undertake to proclaim this Word. . . . Theological speech is taught its content by exegesis and dogmatics, and it is given its form through the experiences of whatever psychology, sociology or linguistics may be most trustworthy at a given moment. . . . Practical theology is studied in order to seek and to find, to learn and to practise, this speech that is essential to the proclamation of the community in preaching and teaching, in worship and evangelisation.[3]

It is evident that Barth, like Schleiermacher, viewed practical theology exclusively as a function of the church and not as an autonomous discipline.[4] But, unlike Schleiermacher, he did not see it as the 'crown of theological studies': for him it was simply a means, albeit an indispensable means, to more effective preaching of the Word. Practical theology is regarded essentially as a prescriptive discipline, because its primary objective is to equip the preacher with the correct tools for preaching the Word.

Sociology is assigned an ancillary role within this understanding of practical theology. At the most, it is able to give theological speech its form: it cannot alter its contents in any way. From Barth's other writings, it is evident that he would have been loathe to admit that an analysis of the social context of theology could in any way affect our understanding of theology. For him contemporary plausibility structures would have been irrelevant. Instead, he admitted only that sociology can exercise an ancillary role in relation to theological speech. Sociology merely provides the practical theologian with a useful tool.

It should be stressed that there is nothing methodologically improper about assigning an ancillary role to sociology *vis-à-vis* practical theology. Ferdinand Boulard was quite happy to see 'religious sociology' in France as an 'auxiliary science of pastoral policy', arguing that 'it is at the service of pastoral theology, which directs the work of the Church towards "the edification

107

of the Body of Christ", by making available a better understanding of human milieus and their influence upon the behaviour of the individuals who live in them'.[5] Boulard's work is certainly open to criticism, but not, I believe, at this point.[6] It is nevertheless important to recognise that, given Barth's and Boulard's prescriptive understandings of practical theology, sociology is accorded an ancillary and not an integral role.

On the other hand, Seward Hiltner's understanding of practical theology, although still prescriptive, does appear to allow the social sciences an integral role—and this may be its weakness. Hiltner divides the theological discipline into two types of field; the 'logic-centred' field and the 'operation-centred' field. Whereas systematic theology belongs to the first, practical theology belongs to the second. He defines the latter as, 'that branch of theological knowledge and inquiry that brings the shepherding perspective to bear upon all the operations and functions of the church and the minister, and then draws conclusions of a theological order from reflection on these observations'.[7] Thus, like Schleiermacher, he locates practical theology within the context of the church's work, but, unlike Schleiermacher, he maintains that the discipline (and along with it the social sciences, from which it derives important insights) not only follows from, but also contributes directly to, systematic theology. In effect, the social sciences are given a determinative role *vis-à-vis* both practical theology and theology in general.

Whatever the particular merits of this understanding of practical theology as such, it is apparent that it risks a conflation of theology with the social sciences, which may do justice to neither discipline.[8] The social sciences are used, not simply to analyse the social context of practical theology, but actually to determine its nature. If only Hiltner had been content with a more modest appreciation of the social sciences as ancillary to practical theology, then his prescriptive understanding of the latter would not have faced this difficulty. However, given that he does have this prescriptive understanding, his allocation of an integral role to the social sciences raises serious methodological problems.

(b) *Prescriptive Christian Ethics*: Within much contemporary

108

Christian ethics there is a parallel prescriptive understanding of the discipline. Proponents of normative, situational or even some contextual ethics, apparently agree that the primary function of Christian ethics is to be concerned with decision-making and eventually to offer 'solutions' to particular ethical dilemmas. Just as many would appear to regard practical theology as the discipline which attempts to resolve problems of praxis (and usually church praxis), similarly, many would appear to regard Christian ethics as the discipline concerned to resolve problems of morality.

Perhaps this is most evident in the instance of situation-ethics. So, for example, Joseph Fletcher offers the following brief account of this approach to ethics:

> The situationist enters into every decision-making situation fully armed with the ethical maxims of his community and its heritage, and he treats them with respect as illuminators of his problems. Just the same he is prepared in any situation to compromise them or set them aside *in the situation* if love seems better served by doing so.[9]

Fletcher contrasts this approach to ethics with 'legalism' on the one hand and 'antinomianism' on the other. In the former approach 'one enters every decision-making situation encumbered with a whole apparatus of prefabricated rules and regulations':[10] in the latter, 'one enters into the decision-making situation armed with no principles or maxims whatsoever, to say nothing of rules'.[11] In all three approaches to ethics, then, Fletcher apparently believes that the central focus is upon the individual confronted with problematic decision-making. Significantly, his characteristic method of commending situation-ethics involves the exegesis of an exceptional paradigm. The latter usually concentrates upon the individual (rather than upon society at large) faced with a seemingly intransigent moral dilemma. It is the primary objective of situation-ethics to resolve such a dilemma, albeit always taking into account the idiosyncrasies of particular situations.

The academic reponse to Fletcher's account of situation-ethics has been enormous—few other works in Christian ethics have created such widespread interest and criticism in the

109

theological world. However, an examination of all the weaknesses that have been attributed to it would not be relevant here.[12] What is relevant, though, is the observation that much of the response to situation-ethics, whether positive or negative, has itself concentrated upon the individual confronted with problematic decision-making. In so far as this is the case, both situation-ethics and the response to it may be depicted as prescriptive.

A single example of this may be given. In his detailed critique of situation-ethics, Paul Ramsey suggests that, in so far as 'agapism' presents Christian ethics with an adequate model, a combination of normative and situation-ethics is necessary if the latter is to be accepted:

> It can be shown that a proper understanding of the moral life will be one in which Christians determine what we ought to do in very great measure by determining which rules of action are most love-embodying, but that there are also always situations in which we are to tell what we should do by getting clear about the facts of that situation and then asking what is the loving or the most loving thing to do in it.[13]

Ramsey's eventual position is, of course, more complicated than this, since he holds that the notion of *agape* alone is not adequate for Christian ethics. Instead, he offers a theory of 'mixed agapism', which he sees as 'a combination of *agape* with man's sense of natural justice or injustice which, however, contains an internal asymmetry that I indicate by the expression "love transforming natural justice"'.[14] Nevertheless, it is clear that he accepts Fletcher's account of the fundamental task of Christian ethics as being the study of the individual confronted with problematic decision-making. Even those, like G. R. Dunstan, who have bemoaned precisely this focus within contemporary Christian ethics, themselves tend to become involved in the self-same prescriptive debate.[15]

As with prescriptive understandings of practical theology, the various prescriptive understandings of Christian ethics again tend to relegate the social sciences in general, and sociology in particular, to an ancillary role. Although Fletcher himself makes little use of sociology, his account of situation-ethics does not preclude the sociologist from clarifying given situations in which an ethical decision is subsequently to be taken. Indeed, the assumption that we should get 'clear about the facts' of particular situations before reaching decisions may well imply a prior assumption about the pertinence of disciplines like sociology. By analysing the 'is', 'was', 'will be' or 'could be' of a given situation—but emphatically not the 'ought to be'—the sociologist may be able to exercise an important function in clarification.[16] Indeed, in all but the most normative accounts of Christian ethics sociology may be able to perform this illuminatory, though essentially ancillary, role.

Whilst it may be no criticism of prescriptive understandings of Christian ethics as such, it is important, in this instance also, to recognise that the possibility of sociology becoming integrally related to the discipline, is precluded. Sociology may be afforded a status somewhat higher than the purely utilitarian one suggested by some understandings of practical theology, but it is still not an integral status. At the most, it can analyse the societal features of the situations surrounding moral dilemmas.

Descriptive Understandings of Applied Theology:
Alongside these prescriptive understandings of applied theology, there have been a number of attempts to suggest a more descriptive orientation for the discipline. Within both Christian ethics and practical theology, several scholars have tried to move away from the production of tangible solutions to particular problems and towards a more analytical/critical approach to issues within applied theology. Thus, within Christian ethics, some exponents have suggested a focus upon the moral context or upon the moral actor, rather than upon moral decision-making; whereas, within practical theology, some have argued for an analysis of the relationship between belief and action in all its complexity, rather than an emphasis upon the requirements of belief for action.

(c) *Descriptive Practical Theology*: Amongst those exponents of practical theology who have advocated the abandonment of a post-Schleiermacher understanding,[17] J. A. Whyte, in particular, has argued against a 'hints and tips' for ordinands approach to the discipline. He believes that instead practical theology should become more seriously theoretical:

> Practical theology must understand itself as *the theology of practice*, and as such a properly academic enquiry. The subject matter of this enquiry is not what is *said*, but what is *done*, as an expression of faith. The data for Practical Theology are not the verbal formulations, the ideas, the language in which people express their faith (or their unbelief), for these are the concern of philosophical or systematic theology, but the activities, the practices, the institutions, the structures of life and of relationships which are, or purport to be, the outcome, embodiment or expression of their faith or unbelief.[18]

In addition, Whyte suggests, unlike Schleiermacher, that 'practice' in this context should not be restricted to ecclesiastical practice and that 'faith' should not be viewed solely as Christian faith.

In so far as it is the function of the practical theologian to analyse religious practice as it relates to religious faith, his task would appear to be identical with that of the sociologist of religion. The analysis of correlations between faith and action is, after all, one that specifically belongs to the latter. Yet the two types of analysis would appear to be distinct, in as much as Whyte believes that the practical theologian has an additional critical function. So, for example, he suggests that the theologian might wish to offer a critique, and not simply an analysis, of social change.

Whyte's account of this descriptive/critical understanding of practical theology, in terms of 'the theology of practice', is brief and open-ended. Whilst rejecting the church and Christian faith as the proper context of the discipline, he makes little attempt to relate the descriptive features of his analysis to contemporary sociology of religion, or to specify the critical criteria necessary to differentiate the latter from practical theology. Nevertheless, it is evident that this understanding of the discipline does allow the possibility of a close interaction between it and sociology. Here, sociology is no longer relegated to the role of an ancillary discipline: a closer integration becomes possible.

A similar, though somewhat more developed, understanding

of practical theology as a descriptive/critical discipline is offered by Karl Rahner. Unlike Whyte, however, he does locate it within the context of the church. For Rahner, 'practical theology is that theological discipline which is concerned with the Church's self-actualisation here and now—both that which *is* and that which *ought to be*'.[19] He rejects the view of practical theology which sees it, either as 'a mere hotch-potch of practical consequences' of other theological disciplines, or 'merely as a collection of psychological, didactic, sociological rules of prudence, gained directly from the ordinary practice of the care of souls'.[20] He maintains, instead, that the discipline is both autonomous and thoroughly theoretical:

> The task of practical theology as an original science demands a theological analysis of the particular present situation in which the Church is to carry out the especial self-realisation appropriate to it at any given moment. In order to be able to perform this analysis of the present by means of scientific reflection and to recognise the Church's situation, practical theology certainly needs sociology, political science, contemporary history, etc. To this extent all these sciences are in the nature of ancillary studies for practical theology. However, although the contemporary analysis provided by these profane sciences is necessary and sufficient for its use, it cannot simply draw on it uncritically as though it were already complete and given. Practical Theology must itself critically distil this analysis within a theological and ecclesial perspective, a task which cannot be taken over by any other theological discipline. . . . Beyond the confrontation of the Church's essence with the contemporary situation, practical theology should contain an element of creativity and prophecy and be engaged in critical reflection.[21]

It is evident, then, that, for Rahner, practical theology has two distinct, though interacting, functions. The first of these is a descriptive function. No longer content with a purely prescriptive understanding of the discipline in which the social sciences are used simply as 'tools', he argues that it is legitimately concerned with analysing the contemporary role of the church *vis-à-vis* society. The second function appears to be a critical/prophetic one, less concerned with the church as it 'is' than with the church as it 'ought to be'. Rahner maintains

113

(although he does not elaborate the point) that the social sciences, including sociology itself, are no longer directly relevant to this second function.

Although Rahner refers to sociology as an 'ancillary' discipline in relation to the descriptive function of practical theology, it is clear that it does, in fact, exercise a more integral role than it might under a prescriptive understanding of the discipline. Certainly, in his account, sociological analysis cannot be conflated with practical theology, since the latter has a critical/prophetic function which would usually be considered inappropriate to the former. However, in so far as practical theology is a descriptive discipline and in so far as it is concerned with offering an analysis of the church's self-actualisation in contemporary society, the role of sociology is far from ancillary.

In differing ways, then, the accounts of Whyte and Rahner both present the possibility that sociological analysis may be regarded as a constituent part of practical theology. Further, both apparently differentiate the two disciplines on the basis of the additional critical function of the latter. Whether the descriptive feature of practical theology is seen, with Whyte, as the analysis of correlations between faith and action or, with Rahner, as the analysis of the church's self-actualisation within society, sociological analysis would appear to be directly relevant. Indeed, the analysis of theology as both a dependent and an independent variable within society, suggested in the previous chapters, can now be seen to be an aspect of this descriptive function of practical theology. This is not to claim, of course, either that this descriptive understanding of practical theology is the 'correct' one, or that the purely sociological analysis of theology offered until now *must* be viewed as an aspect of practical theology. It is to claim, more modestly, that, given this particular understanding of practical theology, a sociological analysis of the determinants and significance of theology can now be seen to be an important feature of the discipline.

(d) *Descriptive Christian Ethics*: Although an emphasis upon ethical decision-making and the resolution of particular moral dilemmas would still appear dominant in contemporary Christian ethics, there is also evidence of a more descriptive understanding. A similar emphasis is to be found in general moral philosophy, although, here too, R. W. Hepburn suggests that, 'there have been . . . some reminders that, whether or not rule-obedience may be the most satisfactory analysis of moral language, very different models are quite often in fact held by morally sensitive people—by those, for instance, who see moral endeavour as the realising of a pattern of life or the following out of a pilgrimage'.[22]

One of the most widely known attempts to present Christian ethics as a descriptive, rather than prescriptive, discipline is that of Paul Lehmann. He argues that the Protestant Reformation entailed for ethics, 'the displacement of the prescriptive and absolute formulation of its claims by the contextual understanding of what God is doing in the world to make and to keep human life human'.[23] As a result, 'ethics could now be a *descriptive* discipline, not in contrast to a normative discipline . . . but in the sense of providing an account of the transformation of the concrete stuff of behaviour, i.e., the circumstances, the motivations, and the structures of action, owing to the concrete, personal, and purposeful activity of God'.[24] For Lehmann, the context of Christian, as distinct from non-Christian, ethics is the *koinonia* and the task of Christian ethics is to elaborate the theological basis of this *koinonia* as it relates to its members. The following passage sets out this thesis in more detail:

> When Christian ethics is defined as *the disciplined reflection upon the question and its answer: What am I, as a believer in Jesus Christ and as a member of his church, to do?* the point of departure is neither vague nor neutral. It is not the common moral sense of mankind, the distilled wisdom of the ages. Not that we can ignore this ethical wisdom, but we do not start with it. Instead, the starting point for Christian thinking about ethics is the fact and the nature of the Christian Church. To put it somewhat too sharply: Christian ethics is not concerned with *the good*, but with what I, as a believer in Jesus Christ and as a member of his church, am to do. *Christian ethics, in other words, is oriented toward revelation and not toward morality.*[25]

This radical relocation of Christian ethics, away from ethical decision-making, ethical theories and moral dilemmas and towards its communal and doctrinal basis, has inevitably

115

attracted critics. So, for example, Paul Ramsey maintains that Lehmann's 'descriptive' approach to ethics suffers from two weaknesses. In the first place, it is 'contradicted by the vast difference and dialectical relation between the hidden and the empirical reality of the *koinonia*':[26] it fails to take seriously the discrepancy between the actual church, with its absence of doctrinal purity, and the *koinonia*. And in the second, it tends to yield only vague generalisations about Christian behaviour, not the detailed prescriptions of traditional Christian ethics or moral theology. Whatever its particular weaknesses as an adequate explication of Christian ethics (which are not relevant here), it does represent an important attempt to focus the discipline on the theological variables upon which it depends as a separate and distinct discipline.

A rather different attempt to relocate Christian ethics away from the individual confronted with problematic ethical decision-making is to be found in the writings of David Harned and Stanley Hauerwas. Harned, whilst agreeing with Lehmann that 'the idea of virtue cannot be explored satisfactorily without extensive reference to the Christian community',[27] seeks in his writings to focus upon 'the importance of vision and imagination in human conduct'.[28] Hauerwas' emphasis is similar although he also concentrates on the idea of 'character' as a focus for Christian ethics, rejecting the exclusive 'command-obedience metaphor' of much contemporary ethics. He believes that 'the language of character does not exclude the language of command but only places it in a larger framework of moral experience'.[29] On this understanding of the discipline, there is no longer sole concentration upon problematic decision-making. Hauerwas suggests a descriptive/critical understanding:

> Once ethics is focused on the nature and moral determination of the self, vision and virtue again become morally significant categories. We are as we come to see and as that seeing becomes enduring in our intentionality. We do not come to see, however, just by looking but by training our vision through the metaphors and symbols that constitute our central convictions. How we come to see therefore is a function of how we come to be since our seeing necessarily is determined by how our basic images are embodied by the self—i.e., in our character. Christian ethics

116

is the conceptual discipline that analyses and imaginatively tests the images most appropriate to score the Christian life in accordance with the central conviction that the world has been redeemed by the work and person of Christ.[30]

Two functions, then, are suggested for Christian ethics—the first analytical/descriptive and the second critical/imaginative. As it happens, it is more to philosophy than sociology that Hauerwas turns for this first function, but, in principle, it is arguable that he might have chosen sociology. After all, the latter could analyse the images actually used by Christians in their moral lives and suggest ways in which these images are determined or determinative. Whereas the second function in Hauerwas' analysis belongs exclusively to the discipline of theology, clearly the first does not. Not surprisingly, then, Harned, in particular, makes frequent use of sociologists, such as Berger and sociological concepts, such as that of secularisation.[31]

There begins to emerge the possibility of an integral relationship between sociology and the descriptive function of these understandings of Christian ethics. The object of scrutiny is not so much the general correlation between faith and activity (whether exclusively within the church or not), but rather the specific correlation between faith and moral activity and even between faith and potential moral activity. Practical theology, viewed in these terms, appears as the overall discipline and Christian ethics as the specialised discipline within it. Both are concerned with the relation between faith and action, but the second has a specialised focus on moral action. Sociology, though, is integrally related to both, performing a primary task of analysis. It is the addition of a critical, evaluative element, superimposed upon a purely descriptive analysis, that distinguishes the task of the applied theologian from that of the sociologist.

Sociology Within Applied Theology:
We are now in a position to isolate a number of ways in which sociology may be employed in the discipline of applied theology. These range from the most superficial and ancillary adoption of sociological techniques to an integral use of sociology as itself a function of applied theology.

117

First, sociological techniques may be used to denote *the social context* within which applied theology operates. At the most superficial level this need not greatly affect the discipline. If the exponent of practical theology or Christian ethics is content to communicate to the faithful alone and not to society at large, he may pay scant attention to the social context within which he operates. In this instance sociological techniques may be used *en passant* and with few clear implications for the discipline. Some of the examples of prescriptive applied theology already cited conform closely to this usage. On the other hand, if the applied theologian is concerned with communication and with the plausibility structures apparent within society, then he, like the general theologian,[32] is obliged to take sociological data more seriously.

Secondly, sociology may play an integral role in the analytical part of descriptive/critical applied theology. In assessing specific correlations between faith and activity, the applied theologian may have recourse to analyses of *the social structure of theology*. As already indicated, the specific correlations which are germane to descriptive practical theology and descriptive Christian ethics, coincide, to a large degree, with an account of theology as a dependent and independent sociological variable. Nevertheless, there is an important difference between the two, at the purely analytical level. Whereas the sociologist, in general, may tend to concentrate on the 'is' rather than the 'could be', that is, on the empirical rather than the speculative, the sociologist working within applied theology may be encouraged to give equal attention to both. Provided that he does not confuse the 'could be' with the 'ought to be', his task remains properly sociological.[33] In this way, he will be able to fulfil the condition that applied theology has seldom been content solely with an analysis of existing activity—potential activity has figured prominently as well.

Thirdly, sociology may play an integral role in assessing, but not evaluating, *the social consequences of theology*. It is at this point that the most radical effects of sociology may be felt within applied theology. Precisely because theology is an evaluative and critical discipline, it cannot ignore its social consequences. A necessary element within the 'explication of the "sequelae" of individual religious beliefs' (to return to my original definition of theology) is that this explication is 'critical'. Within descriptive/critical understandings of applied theology this entails a critical evaluation of the effect of faith upon action and of action upon faith. It is at this point that sociology can perform a crucial function in highlighting the social consequences of belief in general and theology in particular. Without itself evaluating these consequences, it can none the less supply an essential element in theology's self-evaluation.

In Chapter 1 I argued that Marx and Engels' *The German Ideology* contains a moral, not simply an analytical, critique of theology. As a result, I maintained that it cannot be used *in toto* as a reliable interpretation of the discipline in terms of the sociology of knowledge. Precisely because the authors dismissed theology, on the grounds that it reflects a division between mental and material behaviour and between one social class and another, their overall argument is sociologically unacceptable. However, from a theological perspective it may have more justification. Within Christian theology, at least, beliefs and explications of beliefs may be partially assessed by the actions that derive from them. Thus, throughout Christian history, 'heresy' was feared, not simply because it represented distorted beliefs, but because it led to distorted actions. 'Orthodoxy', on the other hand, was frequently correlated with 'morally correct behaviour'. It may be no accident that it was both the doctrinal and the moral arguments of *Honest to God* which caused the most immediate impact. Certainly, John Robinson himself believed that many of his critics automatically correlated the two: bad theology, for them, led to bad moral behaviour.[34]

In contrast to the Marxists, Talcott Parsons believes that it is precisely this correlation which differentiates religious belief from philosophical belief. He argues:

> Religious beliefs may . . . be characterised as the non-empirical homologue of ideological beliefs. By contrast with science or philosophy the cognitive interest is no longer primary, but gives way to the evaluative interest. Acceptance of a religious belief is then a commitment to its implementation in action in a sense in which acceptance of a philosophical belief is not. . . . Religious

119

ideas may be speculative in the philosophical sense, but the attitude toward them is not speculative in the sense that 'well, I wonder if it would make sense to look at it this way?'.[35]

For Parsons, then, religious beliefs and even speculative religious ideas (presumably theology) are directly connected with religious action. Unlike philosophical beliefs, they cannot simply be 'speculative'.

From the theological perspective, it is possible that an evaluation of the social consequences of particular theological ideas and movements might become a major element in a test of their theological truth. Thus, alongside the traditional philosophical and historical tests of theological truth, an additional socio-theological test might be set. In such a test sociology would perform a major function in delineating the actual and potential consequences of these ideas and movements. The final evaluation of these consequences would, of course, rely on extra-sociological criteria. Nevertheless, their delineation would depend entirely upon sociology.

This point is so crucial that it is worth taking an example from one of the few theologians to take it seriously. In his 'theological reading of sociology', Gregory Baum became convinced that, 'the sociological tradition contains basic truth absent from philosophical and theological thought, truth that actually modifies the very meaning of philosophy and theology'.[36] In particular, his socio-theological analysis and critique of the theological roots of anti-Semitism provides an important example of a study of the social consequences of theology.

Together with a number of other analysts,[37] Baum sees a basis for anti-Semitism within Christianity in certain interpretations of the New Testament. He argues that, 'almost from the beginning, the Christian church projected the critical preaching of Jesus, especially his denunciations of hypocrisy, legalism and collective blindness, unto the scribes and Pharisees, the temple priests, and the undefined collectivity called the Jews'.[38] On the basis of certain texts—notably, Matthew 23, Galatians 3 and 4 and John 5 and 8—anti-Semitism soon became established in the early church, despite the latter's obviously Jewish heritage:

The polemics of the New Testament against the Pharisees

distorts the nature and function of this group of men in the history of Israel. Recent scholarship has brought out the spiritual and humanistic character of the Pharisee revolution. While Jesus himself and possibly his early disciples used harsh, prophetic language to denounce the corrupting trends in the religion of their own people, later Christian preachers, speaking no longer out of an identification with Israel but out of a situation of conflict with the Synagogue, repeated the same words as a judgement pronounced by outsiders on the religion of Israel. In this manner, Jesus' prophetic exhortations acquired a different meaning: they were used as a weapon against the Pharisees and eventually against the entire Jewish people.[39]

Well aware of the contemporary evidence, suggesting a positive correlation between anti-Semitism and certain types of religious belief,[40] Baum advances the additional sociological analysis that it was a change in social context which first introduced anti-Semitism into Christianity. Further, he suggests that events like Hegel's identification of 'alienating religion' with Judaism, 'perpetuated an image of a living people that created prejudice and contempt for this people and gave rise to the desire to see their religion suppressed'.[41]

Up to this point in his argument, Baum uses the analytical framework of sociology to identify the social consequences of belief. However, it is soon evident that he is also offering a theological critique in terms of 'alienation'—understanding the latter more in theological, than sociological, terms. Further, reflecting the results of his analysis back on to systematic theology, he argues that it must, in turn, be framed in a manner that avoids the recurrence of anti-Semitism. He argues this forcibly in the following passage:

> Auschwitz should be a turning point for Christian self-understanding. It reveals to us the power of social and religious pathologies. It brings to light the dreadful consequences of the destructive trends in religion. *Corruptio optimi pessima.* What Christians are summoned to do—and this is part of the purpose of this book—is to confront the structures of oppression and the symbols legitimating injustices in the Christian tradition.[42]

The details of Baum's argument are less important than its overall structure. Using sociology to identify the social

121

consequences of particular Christian beliefs, he uses theology to evaluate them. Then he applies these evaluated social consequences directly back to theology itself, suggesting christological and soteriological modifications that can counter them in the future. Sociology is thus afforded a crucial role in this radical test of theological truth.

Finally, sociology may be afforded an integral role in analysing *shared patterns of interaction within Christian ethics*—a role that is not confined to descriptive/critical understandings of the discipline. Even the briefest survey of contemporary Christian ethics, suggests that it is characterised by a considerable degree of pluralism. In recent years, normative, antinomian, situationalist, contextualist, prescriptive, descriptive/critical, Catholic, Protestant, ecumenical and many other understandings of Christian ethics have all been offered. Confronted with this apparent pluralism, it has become extremely difficult to specify any common factor which justifies the single label of 'Christian' ethics.[43] Even Lehmann's contention that the specifically Christian feature of Christian ethics is its location within the *koinonia* is inadequate at the empirical level, since it is clear that several exponents of the discipline do not wish to restrict it in this way. From the sociological perspective, the only feature which the various approaches to Christian ethics may have in common and which distinguishes them from moral philosophy, is a tendency to consider theological factors just as relevant to a moral situation as purely ethical or social ones. Accordingly, the sociologist working within the discipline could construct an account of the way social, ethical and theological variables interact, potentially and actually, in a given moral situation. This would not pretend to be a 'new' approach to Christian ethics: it would not be yet another means of exploring the relevance of Christianity to morality. It would rather supply an analytical framework for viewing some of the empirical and potential factors involved in various understandings of the discipline. A focus upon shared patterns of interaction, between otherwise conflicting approaches, might help to clarify their common claim to be Christian ethics.

This essentially sociological approach to Christian ethics is more holistic than the other uses of sociology within applied theology. It centres, less upon theology seen as the 'explication of the "sequelae" of individual religious beliefs', than upon it viewed as the 'explication of the correlations and interactions between religious beliefs in general'. Like the sociology of ethics in general,[44] it would in part require an analysis in terms of the social determinants and social significance of the discipline *vis-à-vis* society at large. For convenience this might be termed 'external' analysis. However, in so far as an analysis of Christian ethics would require an examination of the theological, ethical and social variables interacting, both actually and potentially, within the discipline, it would clearly differ from a sociology of ethics in general. The peculiar problems, then, attached to 'Christian' ethics require a different sort of analysis, which, again for convenience, might be termed 'internal' analysis.

Internal Analysis and Christian Responses to War:
A brief example should help to clarify the way in which this 'internal' analysis might operate. The recurrent theme, revolving around Christian responses to the ethical issue of war, provides an appropriate and illuminating case-study.

The analyses, provided in Chapters 2 and 4, already constitute part of an 'external' analysis of Christian responses to war. Thus, the examination of the social determinants responsible for the formation of just-war theories in the post-Constantinian churches on the one hand, and that of the social significance of pacifist theologies on the other, can be viewed as part of the descriptive function of applied theology. A descriptive/critical practical theology would wish to go beyond a simple correlation of theology and action and produce a critique, in theological terms, of actual or potential reactions to theology in this context, but it might, at least, start from such sociological analysis. Similarly, a descriptive/critical Christian ethics would go beyond a correlation between theology and specifically moral activity in this context and itself offer a theological critique, but it too would start with this or something like it. The differences here are not so great as to demand a separate elaboration.

The task of 'internal' analysis, though, would be rather different, so it is worth focusing summarily upon it. Here the

123

sociologist is required to set out the actual *and* potential interactions between theological, ethical and social variables inherent in Christian responses to war. It is worth pointing out *en passant* that the latter form particularly interesting data for both 'external' and 'internal' analysis. Certainly, Charles Raven believed that this area of research provides striking subject matter for the analysis of 'the relationship of belief to practice, of the Christian faith to the problems of individual and social ethics'.[45]

Amongst the items to be considered in an analysis of potentially relevant theological variables in this context, the following seven would have to be included. First, images of God might be relevant to differing responses to war. Thus, an image of God, framed in terms of the concept of justice, might invoke a rather different response to one framed in terms of love. Certainly, the pacifist theologian Raven tended to stress the love of God,[46] whereas the just-war theorist Paul Ramsey argues for the notion of 'love transforming natural justice'.[47] Secondly, attitudes towards the Bible may be relevant. The evident militarism of the Old Testament contrasts sharply with the apparent pacifism of the New Testament, and differing theologians may be inclined to stress one, rather than the other, to confirm their particular responses to war. It is relevant to note here that William Temple accused Raven of being a Marcionite for this reason, and Raven, in turn, stressed what he felt to be the incontrovertible evidence of the Gospels.[48] The issue that is raised here is not just the relative emphasis that the theologian places on the Old or New Testament, but his attitude to biblical authority as a whole.[49] These first two variables are themselves interlinked, in so far as the concept of justice might be thought more typical of the Old Testament and love of the New Testament: particular images of God might, as a consequence, depend upon particular attitudes to the Bible.

The third and fourth variables—christology and soteriology—may also be interlinked and dependent, in turn, upon attitudes to the Bible and even upon images of God. That christology is relevant might be adumbrated from a comparison of the incarnational christology of selective militarists, like Karl Barth or William Temple, with the more inspirational approach to christology of Raven—Temple, at least, suspected Raven of Apollinarianism.[50] Soteriology, too, would appear to be relevant: it has already been suggested that Raven found a theological basis for pacifism in the notion of *Imitatio Christi*.[51] Understandings of the atonement, which do not presuppose a close correlation between the behaviour of Christ and that of Christians, would not necessarily impose the same pattern. Thus, connecting these two variables, an understanding of christology in terms of the radical uniqueness of Christ and an understanding of soteriology in terms of a radical discontinuity between Christ and Christians, might support militarist positions more effectively than would opposite understandings. In addition, since no single christological or soteriological model has a monopoly in the New Testament, differing theologians have tended to stress differing features of it and, in turn, have supported their conclusions with differing images of God.

Fifthly and sixthly, one might isolate the variables of ecclesiology and eschatology and suggest interconnections. In Chapter 2 it was suggested that differing responses to war may, in part, reflect differing types of religious organisation. Thus, whilst selective militarism characterises the church, thorough-going pacifism is only possible for the sect. It cannot, of course, be claimed that all sects are pacifist-oriented (the majority are not) or that all church members are selective militarists (Raven, after all, was not) but it is possible that differences between ecclesiastical and sectarian theologies may be relevant to an understanding of their differing responses to war. At issue are their respective responses to the state—arguably a differentiating factor amongst sects themselves.[52] Thus, their radical opposition to society may encourage the Jehovah's Witnesses to oppose particular societal wars. Likewise, as was argued in Chapter 4, their emphasis upon an imminent *parousia* makes the espousal of any human war even less likely. In contrast, it was argued in Chapter 3 that churches tend to differ very little, if at all, from society at large, on issues of public morality—and even on issues of sexual morality, their views tend eventually to conform to those of the general population. Similarly, churches seldom maintain an imminent and cataclysmic eschatology in radical opposition to the state or human wars. Interconnections with other theological variables are also apparent, since it is evident, for example, that the sectarian and apocalyptic features of Jehovah's Witness theology owe much to its particular emphasis on, and understanding of, the apocalyptic parts of the Old and New Testaments, and in turn on its images of a God of wrath and on the particular kind of salvation that he effects.

Finally, theological anthropology might be suggested as a relevant variable in the context of Christian responses to war. A heavy stress on the fallen nature of man may foster a belief both in the inevitability of war[53] and in the necessity of potentially violent deterrence.[54] On theological grounds (owing much to certain understandings of the Bible) man is viewed as fallen and consequently as inherently warlike. Conversely, the representative pacifism of the Quakers and of individuals within the churches,[55] suggests a different theological anthropology, according to which man is viewed as essentially redeemable. Again, it is not surprising to find that Temple suspected Raven of Pelagianism.[56] Further, the possible effectiveness of non-violent action maintained by some churchmen, also suggests a doctrine of man's essential redeemability, rather than his intransigent imprisonment in original sin.[57]

Without claiming that this list of theological variables in this context is exhaustive, it can already be seen that there emerges a complex pattern of potential interconnections. However, this complexity is compounded by the addition of ethical and social variables into the analysis. So, a variety of ethical theories are evident within Christian responses to war. The response of the contemporary Quakers would appear to contain a mixture of a radical appeal to conscience and a deal of pragmatism: their opposition to human wars does not take the normative stance of some thoroughgoing pacifists. Whilst feeling unable to fight, on grounds of conscience, they have served as medical orderlies (thereby compromising their position by assisting the 'war effort'—in the view of those following a more normative approach)[58]—in the process of which they have 'borne witness' to the ideal of pacifism.[59] The adoption of nuclear weapons as deterrents against war, has been justified by other Christians in terms of a common-good theory of ethics.[60] Amongst Roman

126

Catholic moral theologians natural law has traditionally been used as a justification of wars of defence.[61] The Protestant theologian Albert Schweitzer, on the other hand, justified his thoroughgoing pacifism in terms of the natural principle of 'reverence for life'. Again, the notion of 'respect for persons' is often invoked as a principle, in the formation of either just-war theories, or in a theory of thoroughgoing pacifism.

As the previous discussions of Christian responses to war have suggested, the sociologist is also confronted with a complex set of social variables. Not only does he have to take into account the four levels at which theological variables may operate—theologians, preachers, listeners and outsiders—and the three approaches he may adopt when examining the social determinants of theology—socio-cultural, socio-political and socio-ecclesiastical—but, he must also take into account a wide variety of different factors, like the type of armaments to be adopted, the proximity of aggression, the possibility of victory and so on.

An 'internal' analysis of the theological, ethical and social variables apparent, actually and potentially, within Christian responses to war, presents the sociologist with a bewildering series of interconnections. Whereas it is possible to trace these connections, in the instance of a single theologian like Raven, or in the case of a relatively uniform religious organisation like that of the Jehovah's Witnesses, any overall map of Christian responses to war would prove extraordinarily complex. Nevertheless, a feature common to all Christian ethics and differentiating them from ethics in general, would appear to be their use of the theological variables already outlined. Potentially, at least, these seven theological variables would appear determinative in all Christian responses to war. An empirical demonstration of this, under 'external' analysis, would, of course, be difficult. Yet an 'internal' analysis suggests this as a possibility.

It might seem that this type of analysis commits a category error, since it apparently suggests that ethical 'oughts' are directly derivable from theological 'is's'. In part, this is the criticism that is often directed at Lehmann's contextualism—that he telescopes the discipline of Christian ethics, by deriving

127

codes of behaviour from doctrinal positions, without the intervention of ethical theories.[62] Whether or not this criticism is correct in the instance of Lehmann, it is hardly relevant to the present analysis. There is no suggestion here that theological variables directly determine ethical decisions, but merely, that in the complex interaction of theological, ethical and social variables each determines the range of possibilities open to the Christian responding to war. Thus, an image of God as love, does not in itself determine whether a Christian should be a thoroughgoing pacifist or a selective militarist, since both might claim it as a principle—the former believing that a loving God wishes him to abandon all war and the latter that the same God wishes him to defend his country. Yet both would insist that they could not respond to war in a way which denied that God is love. Further, this principle, in combination with other theological and ethical variables, does become determinative—as the example of Charles Raven indicates. Similarly, the particular mixture of sectarian, eschatological, biblical and soteriological beliefs of the Jehovah's Witnesses does considerably restrict their possible responses to war. Without being declared pacifists, they are nevertheless unable to take part in human wars. Here, theological positions have demonstrably limited the possibilities of ethical choice, without deriving ethical prescriptions directly from doctrinal beliefs. So, as Talcott Parsons suggests, value-orientations are 'guided' by beliefs, even if they are not wholly determined by them.[63]

This brief case-study serves to demonstrate the sheer complexity of such a sociological account of Christian ethics. That it is necessary is evident from the considerable pluralism within the contemporary discipline. Without providing yet another way of 'doing' Christian ethics, it might at least help to clarify its function and role. This, in itself, would make a major contribution to applied theology as a genuinely theoretical academic discipline.

7

Theology—An Interactionist Perspective

THROUGHOUT THIS book it has been maintained that, whilst a separate focus upon the determinants and significance of theology is procedurally unavoidable, it none the less distorts the role that theology actually plays within society. At several points in the text I have indicated that this role presents the sociologist with a complex web of interactions.

It would do less than justice to the material to conclude without some indication of the way these interactions function. I have not attempted a complete account of theology from the perspective of the sociology of knowledge—for example, I have presented no analysis of differing patterns of theological socialisation or education and no explanatory account of the social origins of theology. Nevertheless, an interpretation of theology as both a dependent and an independent variable and an analysis of the complex interactions between these two possibilities, do constitute the basic core of a sociological understanding of theology.

The main justification for focusing separately on the social determinants and the social significance of theology is that such focus presents the sociologist with an empirically manageable area of study. One of the criticisms often levelled at the sociology of knowledge is that it is insufficiently rigorous.[1] It has tended to generate, neither empirically testable hypotheses, in the case of contemporary material, nor rigorously critical theories, in the instance of historical material. To avoid such generalities, I have maintained that an, admittedly distorting, focus does provide the sociologist of knowledge with a clearly defined task, which is suceptible to critical analysis.

Whilst an analysis based on an interactionist approach to theology might prove too complex to sustain rigorous inspection, the evidence itself does seem to point ideally to the necessity of such analysis. Thus, the sociologist is presented with a dilemma; a study of theology separately, in terms of its social determinants and social significance, would appear to produce sociologically plausible results, but the evidence exposed, in the course of such study, would seem to indicate a complex web of interactions between theology and society, which even the most exhaustive sociological analysis might fail adequately to unravel. Given the current immaturity of sociological accounts of theology, the more rigorous, although necessarily focused, study is to be preferred.

Even a brief reappraisal of Weber's thesis, contained in *The Protestant Ethic and the 'Spirit' of Capitalism*,[2] is sufficient to indicate the complexity of the interactions between theology and society. In contrast to Marx and Engels who, as has already been suggested, viewed contemporary theology as an expression of the bourgeoisie within a situation of elitist capitalism, Weber offered the possibility that specific features within Calvinist theology may have contributed to the rise of capitalism within the West. Thus, while Marx and Engels tended to view theology merely as a dependent variable within society, Weber entertained the possibility that it acted as both a dependent and an independent variable. Seemingly, the two accounts of the relationship between theology and capitalism are mutually exclusive; for one, theology is seen as the expression of capitalism, while for the other, it is seen as a contributory feature to the rise of capitalism.

But opposing the two theories in this way is too simplistic. Had Weber continued his analysis of the relationship between theology and capitalism, he too might have adopted a part of Marx and Engels' thesis. It is clear that he applied the contribution of theology to the rise of capitalism, not to its subsequent maintenance. The peculiar moral qualities most apposite to the spirit of capitalism, once fostered by Calvinist theology, could survive without their religious roots. As a result, it is possible that Weber could have maintained intact his thesis about the contribution of theology to the rise of capitalism and yet still have claimed, with Marx and Engels, that contemporary theology is basically an expression of capitalism. On this understanding, theology would be accorded a determinative role in fostering the rise of capitalism and a determined role in being influenced by this capitalism, once established. Theoretically, at least, there is no necessary conflict between these two analyses of theology *vis-à-vis* capitalism.

Confusingly, though, Weber *does* begin his analysis of theological factors involved in the rise of capitalism within the West, with an observation of 'the fact that business leaders and owners of capital, as well as the higher grades of skilled labour, and even more the higher technically and commercially trained personnel of modern enterprises, are overwhelmingly Protestant'.[3] Although this observation is not fully integrated into his theory as it develops, we do appear to be presented with the possibility—itself subjected to considerable contemporary research[4]—that differences between Catholics and Protestants, in relation to capitalism, may still persist, despite the apparently 'autonomous' nature of the latter. In so far as these apparent differences are themselves dependent upon theological differences, the sociologist is presented with a daunting task of empirical analysis. Having carefully identified the various features within Calvinist theology which Weber held to be peculiarly influential—notably the concepts of vocation, predestination, inner-worldly asceticism and sanctification[5]—he is confronted with the possibility that theology may have contributed to the rise of capitalism and to existing differences of attitude within capitalism and at the same time may have become an expression of capitalism.

Even if the specific theories of either Weber, or Marx and Engels, on the relationship between theology and capitalism are rejected by the sociologist, he still cannot ignore them, since it is evident that a new element, which is not dependent on their validity, has entered the situation. Certain strands within contemporary theology have actually incorporated Weberian or Marxian analyses into their self-understanding. It is precisely at this point that the complex web of interactions between theology and society becomes apparent. Not only is theology viewed as 'a highly complex, many-levelled, ambivalent phenomenon' (as Baum depicts religion)[6] which is capable of a variety of different responses to society at large, but it is seen also as able to assimilate ostensibly unflattering analyses of itself actually into itself.

So, in his theological critique of sociology, Baum instances the object of the Weberian thesis as an example of 'creative religion', depicting it as follows:

> An original, creative, religious breakthrough took place in Calvinistic Christianity. God's call was experienced as a secular calling. Christians experienced the meaning and power of the gospel in their dedication to hard work and personal enterprise, and they regarded the success of their undertakings as God's approval and blessing. This new spirituality removed the religious obstacles to capitalistic expansion, for in the Middle Ages the Church had not only regarded as gravely sinful the taking of interest on money loaned, but had also held up contemplation, other worldliness, patience in one's providential position, and even elected poverty as the ideals to be followed by the most dedicated Christians.[7]

Similarly, it is evident that a number of contemporary theologians have sought to develop 'syntheses' between Marxism and Christianity and even to adopt Marxian concepts into their understanding of the theological discipline.[8] Within this situation, it would seem that, not only is sociological analysis an important means of investigating the complex interaction between theology and society, but is itself a part of that interaction. The Weberian and Marxian theories themselves act as independent variables in the relationship between theology and capitalism.

This new element raises crucial problems for Marx and Engels' analysis of the social determinants of theology. It would seem that it is no longer possible to identify theology, *tout court*, as the product of a spurious division between mental and material behaviour and as the expression of the bourgeoisie, since this analysis is already adopted within certain understandings of theology. Certainly, one of the aspects of some forms of 'liberation theology', as it has been developed in South America and Africa, is that it is self-consciously a proletarian product seeking to effect political change. Such an understanding of theology is clearly based neither on a division between material and mental behaviour, nor on an expression of ruling class attitudes.

The convolutions of this analysis become even greater if the possibility is also entertained that, not only may sociological analysis play a determinative role *vis-à-vis* theology, but also that theology may have played a determinative role in the initial framing of this analysis. Roderick Martin's suggestion that Marx's concept of alienation, Weber's notion of disenchantment and Durkheim's idea of social disintegration, all have theological roots,[9] brings the analysis round in a full circle. As I have argued elsewhere,[10] Martin believes that an adequate understanding of early sociology must see that 'it drew its theoretical concepts from sources as diverse as Christian theology, enlightenment rationalism, German idealism, the conservative reaction to the French and industrial revolutions, and many others'.[11] If this suggestion is allowed, then the task of unravelling the interaction between theology and society becomes even more daunting.

The full range of complexities would only be uncovered by the sociologist of knowledge studying theology as a multi-layered activity, determined and determining a multilayered society through a series of varied interactions. Inevitably, any such understanding overrules simplistic, mono-causal explanations, whether in terms of theology being *tout court* the product of a particular class or a particular mode of behaviour, or in terms of theology being an autonomous, determinative discipline, owing nothing to social phenomena.

Whilst it might be impossible to achieve a thoroughgoing account of theology in these terms, it is possible to offer an ideal paradigm for a sociological understanding of theology. Like all ideal paradigms or ideal types, it is an abstraction which corresponds, only in places, to empirical actualities. Again, like them, it offers the sociologist a stylised framework for studying the interactions between theology and society and, in particular, it offers a stylised chronology. Nevertheless, given a rigorous account both of the social determinants and of the social significance of theology, it does present the sociologist with a paradigm for setting these accounts into a more interactionist perspective.

133

In terms of this paradigm, theology would appear as a thoroughly determined discipline, originating from and being maintained by, social factors. Nevertheless, theology, once socially constructed and maintained, in turn determines society at any one of four levels—theologians, preachers, listeners and outsiders—in proportion to their contact with the discipline. In turn, society, once determined by theology, acts as a fresh determinant itself on theology—again at the four levels and in proportion to their contact with the discipline.

As the full range of complex interactions is explored, this circular paradigm is susceptible to endless repetition. Yet, as a heuristic device, it presents a stylised over-view of the detailed, but focused, analyses that have been offered in this book. It has been my argument that these offer a rich source of largely unexplored data to the sociologist and to the theologian. Hopefully, an analysis of theology, in terms of the sociology of knowledge, can generate fresh insights for the followers of both disciplines.

Notes

INTRODUCTION

1. see Ernst Troeltsch, *The Social Teaching of the Christian Churches*, Vols I & II, Harper, 1960, H. R. Niebuhr, *The Social Sources of Denominationalism*, World Publishing Co., 1929, D. Bonhoeffer, *Sanctorum Communio*, Collins, 1963.
2. Peter L. Berger, *A Rumour of Angels*, Pelican, 1969, p. 47.

CHAPTER 1

1. e.g. Gregory Baum, *Religion and Alienation: A Theological Reading of Sociology*, Paulist Press, 1975.
2. e.g. Murdo Ewen Macdonald, *The Call to Communication*, St Andrews, 1975, Dennis Nineham, 'A Partner for Cinderella?', in ed. Morna Hooker and Colin Hickling, *What About the New Testament?*, SCM, 1975, and Charles Davis, *The Temptations of Religion*, London, 1973.
3. see ed. J. E. Curtis and J. W. Petras, *The Sociology of Knowledge: A Reader*, Duckworth, 1970, Introduction, and Robert K. Merton, *Social Theory and Social Structure*, The Free Press, 1957, pp. 460f.
4. Peter L. Berger, *The Precarious Vision*, Doubleday, 1961.
5. cf. Bryan S. Turner, *Weber and Islam*, Routledge & Kegan Paul, 1974, pp. 1–4.
6. cf. Betty Scharf, *The Sociological Study of Religion*, Hutchinson, 1970, p. 33.
7. cf. Roland Robertson, *The Sociological Interpretation of Religion*, Blackwell, 1970, p. 47f.
8. see ed. Curtis and Petras, *op. cit,*. pp. 7–8.
9. Francis Bacon, 'On the Interpretation of Nature and the Empire of Man', in ed. Curtis and Petras, *op. cit.*, p. 96.
10. Karl Marx and Frederick Engels, *The German Ideology*, ed. C. J. Arthur, Lawrence & Wishart, 1970, p. 47.
11. see Karl Marx and Frederick Engels, *On Religion*, Lawrence & Wishart, 1958.
12. Marx and Engels, *The German Ideology, op. cit.*, p. 47.
13. *ibid.*, p. 64.
14. *ibid.*, p. 65.
15. *ibid.*, p. 61.
16. *ibid.*
17. Robin Gill, *The Social Context of Theology*, Mowbrays, 1975, p. 20.
18. Karl Mannheim, *Ideology and Utopia*, Routledge & Kegan Paul, 1936, p. 238.
19. *ibid.*, p. 50.
20. *ibid.*, p. 68.
21. *ibid.*, p. 69.
22. see Peter Hamilton, *Knowledge and Social Structure*, Routledge & Kegan Paul, 1974, p. 75f.
23. Max Scheler, 'The Sociology of Knowledge: Formal Problems', in ed. Curtis and Petras, *op. cit.*, p. 175.

24. Mannheim, *op. cit.*, p. 250.
25. *ibid.*, p. 39.
26. see Max Scheler, 'On the Positivistic Philosophy of the History of Knowledge and Its Law of Three Stages', in ed. Curtis and Petras, *op. cit.*, pp. 161–9.
27. Mannheim, *op. cit.*, pp. 254–5.
28. see Hamilton, *op. cit.*, pp. 120–1, and Peter L. Berger and Thomas Luckmann, *The Social Construction of Reality*, Penguin, 1971, p. 20f.
29. Mannheim, *op. cit.*, p. 71.
30. see Hans Speier, 'The Social Determination of Ideas', in ed. Curtis and Petras, *op. cit.*, pp. 263–81.
31. Mannheim, *op. cit.*, pp. 40–1.
32. Talcott Parsons, 'Introduction' to Max Weber, *The Sociology of Religion*, Methuen, 1965, p. xxiii.
33. Merton, *op. cit.*
34. *ibid.*
35. cf. Bernard Barber, 'Toward a New View of the Sociology of Religion', in ed. Lewis A. Coser, *The Idea of Social Structure*, Harcourt Brace Jovanovich, 1975, pp. 103–16.
36. Scheler, *op. cit.*
37. see Hamilton, *op. cit.*, p. 81.
38. Werner Stark, *The Sociology of Knowledge*, Routledge & Kegan Paul, 1958, pp. 48–9.
39. *ibid.*, p. 49.
40. Berger and Luckmann, *op. cit.*, p. 24.
41. Stark, *op. cit.*, p. 159.
42. cf. Hamilton, *op. cit.*, p. 87.
43. Stark, *op. cit.*, p. 346.
44. Werner Stark, *The Sociology of Religion*, Routledge & Kegan Paul, 1966–9, Vols I–V.
45. Stark, *The Sociology of Knowledge, op. cit.*, pp. 20–1.
46. cf. Barber, *op. cit.*
47. see Weber, *op. cit.*, p. 23f.
48. Berger and Luckmann, *op. cit.*, p. 26.
49. see Alasdair MacIntyre, *Against the Self-Images of the Age*, Duckworth, 1971, see also J. Habermas, *Knowledge and Human Interests*, Beacon Press, 1971, cf. Ninian Smart, *The Science of Religion and the Sociology of Knowledge*, Princeton University Press, 1975, p. 74f.
50. see Berger and Luckmann, *op. cit.*, p. 25.
51. *ibid.*, pp. 26–7.
52. Hamilton, *op. cit.*, p. 145. cf. Björn Eriksson, *Problems of an Empirical Sociology of Knowledge*, Uppsala, 1975.
53. Berger and Luckmann, *op. cit.*, p. 29.
54. Gill, *op. cit.*, chap. 7.
55. Peter L. Berger, *The Social Reality of Religion*, Penguin, 1973, p. 184.
56. Peter L. Berger, 'Identity as a Problem in the Sociology of Knowledge', in ed. Curtis and Petras, *op. cit.*, p. 377.
57. Berger, *The Social Reality of Religion, op. cit.*, p. 34.
58. cf. Gill, *op. cit.*, p. 37.
59. *ibid.*, p. 27f.

CHAPTER 2

1. ed. Charles Y. Glock and Phillip E. Hammond, *Beyond the Classics: Essays in the Scientific Study of Religion*, Harper & Row, 1973, p. xiii.
2. cf. Ernest Krausz, 'Religion as a Key Variable', in ed. Elizabeth Gittus, *Key Variables in Social Research*, Vol. 1, Heinemann, 1972, and Kevin Clements, 'The Religious Variable', in ed. Michael Hill, *A Sociological Yearbook of Religion in Britain*, SCM, 1971.
3. cf. Talcott Parsons, 'Introduction' to Max Weber, *The Sociology of Religion*, Methuen, 1965.
4. see further, W. S. F. Pickering, *Durkheim on Religion*, Routledge & Kegan Paul, 1975.
5. Emile Durkheim, *The Elementary Forms of the Religious Life*, George Allen & Unwin, 1976.
6. Emile Durkheim, *Suicide*, Routledge & Kegan Paul, 1970, p. 170.
7. *ibid.*
8. cf. Peter L. Berger, *A Rumour of Angels*, Pelican, 1969.
9. e.g. Waldo Beach, *Christian Community and American Society*, Westminster, Philadelphia, 1969, and John Bowker, *The Sense of God*, OUP, 1973—see further, Robin Gill, *The Social Context of Theology*, Mowbrays, 1975, chap. 3.
10. Peter L. Berger, *The Social Reality of Religion*, Penguin, 1973, p. 183.
11. cf. Roland Robertson and Colin Campbell, 'Religion in Britain: the Need for New Research Strategies', *Social Compass*, XIX/2, 1972, and Gary D. Bouma, 'Recent "Protestant Ethic" Research', *Journal for the Scientific Study of Religion*, Vol. 21, No. 2 1973.
12. Peter Brown, *Augustine of Hippo*, Faber & Faber, 1967.
13. see F. W. Dillistone, *Charles Raven: Naturalist, Historian and Theologian*, Hodder & Stoughton, 1975.
14. Peter Brown, *Religion and Society in the Age of Saint Augustine*, Faber & Faber, 1972, p. 133.
15. *ibid.*, pp. 123–4.
16. E. E. Evans-Pritchard, *Witchcraft, Oracles and Magic Among the Azande*, Clarendon Press, 1937, p. 63f.
17. Brown, *op. cit.*, p. 132
18. *ibid.*, p. 135.
19. Gill, *op. cit.*, chap. 6.
20. Bryan Wilson, *Religion in Secular Society*. Pelican, 1969, p. 97.
21. *ibid.*, p. 151.
22. *ibid.*, p. 14, see also Bryan Wilson, *Contemporary Transformations of Religion*, OUP, 1976.
23. Peter L. Berger, *The Social Reality of Religion*, *op. cit.*, p. 168.
24. e.g. David Martin, *The Religious and the Secular*, Routledge & Kegan Paul, 1969: see also A. G. B. Woollard, *Progress: A Christian Doctrine?*, SPCK, 1972, chap. 3.
25. G. E. Swanson, *The Birth of the Gods*, University of Michigan, 1960.
26. Max Weber, *The Sociology of Religion*, Methuen, 1965, p. 23.
27. John Bowker, *The Sense of God*, OUP, 1973, p. 29.
28. Weber, *op. cit.*, pp. 124–5.
29. Robertson, *op. cit.*, p. 207.
30. cf. David Martin, 'The Secularisation Question', *Theology*, Vol. LXXVI, No. 630, Feb. 1973, p. 86.

31. see Scharf, *op. cit.*
32. Bryan Wilson, 'A Typology of Sects', in ed. Roland Robertson, *Sociology of Religion*, Penguin, 1969, p. 363.
33. see Bryan Wilson, *Sects and Society*, Heinemann, 1955.
34. e.g. Susan Budd, *Sociologists and Religion*, Collier-Macmillan, 1973, p. vii.
35. Roland H. Bainton, *Christian Attitudes Toward War and Peace*, Abingdon, 1960, p. 66.
36. *ibid.*, p. 85, cf. Peter Brock, *Pacifism in Europe to 1914*. Princeton University Press, 1972 and Geoffrey Nuttall, *Christian Pacifism in History*, World Without War, 1958.
37. see Charles E. Raven, *Is War Obsolete?*, George Allen & Unwin, 1935, *War and the Christian*, London, 1938, *The Theological Basis of Pacifism*, London, 1952.
38. Charles E. Raven, *Is War Obsolete?*, *op. cit.*, p. 44.
39. *ibid.*, p. 40.
40. see Dillistone, *op. cit.*, p. 437.
41. *ibid.*, p. 220f.
42. cf. Bainton, *op. cit.*, p. 53f.
43. see G. H. C. MacGregor, *The New Testament Basis of Pacifism*, James Clarke, 1936, cf. C. J. Cadoux, *The Early Christian Attitude to War*, London, 1919.
44. Eberhard Welty, *A Handbook of Christian Social Ethics*, Nelson, 1963, Vol. 2, pp. 396–7.
45. T. R. Milford, *The Valley of Decision: the Christian Dilemma in the Nuclear Age*, British Council of Churches, 1961, p. 21. For Ambrose, Augustine and Aquinas see ed. Arthur F. Holmes, *War and Christian Ethics*, Baker, 1975.
46. *ibid.*
47. Welty, *op. cit.*, p. 409.
48. J. Milton Yinger, *The Scientific Study of Religion*, Collier-Macmillan, 1970, p. 465.
49. *ibid.*, p. 460.
50. *ibid.*, p. 467. cf. David Martin, *Pacifism*, Routledge & Kegan Paul, 1965, Brock, *op. cit.*, and Peter Brock, *Twentieth-Century Pacifism*, Van Nostrand Reinhold, 1970.

CHAPTER 3

1. Robin Gill, *The Social Context of Theology*, Mowbrays, 1975, chap. 4.
2. cf. David Martin, 'Ethical Commentary and Political Decision', *Theology*, Oct. 1973, p. 527.
3. cf. V. A. Demant, 'Sociological Factors in the Determination of Christian Morals', in ed. Gerard Irvine, *Christianity in its Social Context*, SPCK, 1967.
4. James T. Richardson and Sandie Wightman, 'Religious affiliation as a predictor of voting behaviour in abortion reform legislation', *Journal for the Scientific Study of Religion*, 1972, pp. 347–59, and James T. Richardson and Sandie Wightman Fox, 'Religion and Voting on Abortion Reform: a follow-up study', *J.S.S.R.*, 1975, pp. 159–64.
5. *ibid.*, 1975, p. 162.
6. *ibid.*, p. 160.
7. *ibid.*, p. 164.
8. though see Bradley Hertel, Gerry E. Hendshot and James W. Grimm,

'Religion and Attitudes Toward Abortion: A Study of Nurses and Social Workers', *J.S.S.R.*, Vol. 13, No. 1, 1974.

9. see Lane Committee, *Report of the Committee on the Working of the Abortion Act*, HMSO, 1974, Vol. 1, p. 794.
10. Const. *Apostolicae Sedis Moderatione*.
11. Canon 63e. C. J. von Hefele, *Histoire de Conciles*, Paris, 1907, Vol. 1, pt 1, p. 256.
12. Canon 21. *ibid.*, p. 323.
13. see Lane Committee, *op. cit.*, Vol. 2, pp. 20–3.
14. see International Planned Parenthood Federation, *European Survey*, March 1973.
15. cf. H. Davis, *Moral and Pastoral Theology*, Sheed & Ward, 1946, Vol. 2, p. 171.
16. e.g. Eberhard Welty, *A Handbook of Christian Social Ethics*, Nelson, 1963, Vol. 1.
17. cf. Lane Committee, *op. cit.*, Vol. 3, pp. 29–30.
18. see G. R. Dunstan, *The Artifice of Ethics*, SCM, 1974, p. 38.
19. *ibid.*, p. 48.
20. The Church Assembly Board of Social Responsibility, *Abortion: an Ethical Discussion*, Church Information Office, 1965, p. 67.
21. *ibid.*, p. 52.
22. Kenneth Child, *Sick Call*, SPCK, 1965, pp. 99–100.
23. *The Abortion Act 1967*, HMSO.
24. cf. Lane Committee, *op. cit.*, Vol. 1.
25. see *ibid.*, and IPPF, *op. cit.*
26. e.g. Dunstan, *op. cit.*
27. see Board of Social Responsibility's Committee for Social Work and the Social Services' *Newsletter*, No. 9, May 1974.
28. *Abortion: an Ethical Discussion, op. cit.*
29. Dunstan, *op. cit.*, p. 87.
30. see Lane Committee, *op. cit.*, and IPPF, *op. cit.*
31. see Lane Committee, *op. cit.*, Vol. 3.
32. see Dunstan, *op. cit.*, p. 87.
33. cf. *ibid.*
34. see World Council of Churches' Office of Family Ministries, *Pastoral Care of those Confronted with Abortion*, Oct. 1975.
35. *ibid.*

CHAPTER 4

1. e.g. Bryan Wilson, *Religion in Secular Society*, Pelican, 1969, Bryan Wilson, *Contemporary Transformations of Religion*, OUP, 1976, and Peter Berger, *The Social Reality of Religion*, Faber & Faber, 1969.
2. cf. E. L. Mascall, *The Secularisation of Christianity*, Libra, 1967.
3. see Bryan S. Turner, 'The Sociological Explanation of Ecumenicalism', in ed. C. L. Mitton, *The Social Sciences and the Churches*, T. & T. Clark, 1972.
4. Peter L. Berger and Thomas Luckmann, *The Social Construction of Reality*, Penguin, 1971.
5. see Berger, *op. cit.*
6. Roger Mehl, *The Sociology of Protestantism*, SCM, 1970, p. 6.
7. *ibid.*, p. 7.
8. *ibid.*, p. 2.

9. M. J. Jackson, *The Sociology of Religion*, Batsford, 1974, pp. 46–7.
10. *ibid.*, p. 47.
11. *ibid.*, p. 40.
12. *ibid.*
13. *ibid.*, p. 50.
14. cf. Michael Hill, *A Sociology of Religion*, Heinemann, 1973.
15. cf. Bryan Wilson, 'The Debate Over "Secularization"', *Encounter*, Oct 1975.
16. cf. Robert Towler, *Homo Religiosus; Sociological Problems in the Study of Religion*, Constable, 1974.
17. see Robin Gill, *The Social Context of Theology*, Mowbrays, 1975, chap. 2.
18. see Charles Y. Glock and Rodney Stark, *Christian Beliefs and Anti-Semitism*, Harper, 1966.
19. see Richard L. Gorsuch and Daniel Aleshire, 'Christian Faith and Prejudice: Review of Research', *Journal for the Scientific Study of Religion*, Vol. 13, No. 3, 1974.
20. Max Weber, *The Protestant Ethic and the 'Spirit' of Capitalism*, Scribner, 1958, p. 187, n. 1.
21. *ibid.*, p. 53.
22. see. Gary D. Bouma, 'Recent "Protestant Ethic" Research', *Journal for the Scientific Study of Religion*, Vol. 21, No. 2, 1973, and ed. Charles Y. Glock and Phillip E. Hammond, *Beyond the Classics? Essays in the Scientific Study of Religion*, Harper & Row, 1973, pp. 113–30.
23. Weber, *op. cit.*, p. 91.
24. Kevin Clements, 'The Religious Variable: Dependent, Independent or Interdependent?', in ed. Michael Hill, *A Sociological Yearbook of Religion in Britain*, SCM, 1971, p. 40.
25. *ibid.*, p. 45.
26. see Kevin Clements, 'The Churches and Social Policy: A Study in the Relationship of Ideology to Action', unpublished Ph.D. Thesis, Victoria University of Wellington, New Zealand, 1970.
27. Gerhard E. Lenski, *The Religious Factor*, Doubleday, 1961.
28. see Bouma, *op. cit.*
29. cf. Michael Hill, *A Sociology of Religion*, Heinemann, 1973.
30. though see Betty Scharf, *The Sociological Study of Religion*, Hutchinson, 1970
31. Gill, *op. cit.*, pp. 4–5.
32. see Roland H. Bainton, *Christian Attitudes Toward War and Peace*, Abingdon, 1960, p. 53f.
33. cf. J. Milton Yinger, *The Scientific Study of Religion*, Macmillan, 1970, p. 466f.
34. Charles E. Raven, *The Theological Basis of Christian Pacifism*, The Fellowship of Reconciliation, 1952.
35. Charles E. Raven, *War and the Christian*, SCM, 1938, p. 21.
36. *ibid.*, cf. Charles E. Raven, *Is War Obsolete?*, George Allen & Unwin, 1935, p. 39f.
37. Raven, *War and the Christian*, *op. cit.*, pp. 48–9.
38. Raven, *The Theological Basis of Christian Pacifism*, *op. cit.*, p. 21.
39. see G. H. C. Macgregor, *The New Testament Basis of Pacifism*, James Clarke, 1936.
40. see Charles E. Raven, *Lessons of the Prince of Peace*, Longmans, Green & Co, 1942.
41. Raven, *The Theological Basis of Christian Pacifism*, *op. cit.*, p. 22.

42. *ibid.*
43. e.g. Eberhard Welty, *A Handbook of Christian Social Ethics*, Nelson, 1963, Vol. 2, pp. 396–7.
44. Werner Stark, *The Sociology of Knowledge*, Routledge & Kegan Paul, 1958, p. 20f.
45. Raven, *War and the Christian*, op. cit., p. 124.
46. Raven, *The Theological Basis of Christian Pacifism*, op. cit., p. 1.
47. Raven, *War and the Christian*, op. cit., pp. 182–3.
48. see Clements, op. cit.
49. see Bryan Wilson, *Religious Sects*, Weidenfeld & Nicolson, 1970, p. 114.
50. see Yinger, op. cit., p. 467, cf. Peter Brock, *Twentieth-Century Pacifism* Van Nostrand Reinhold, 1970.
51. Wilson, op. cit., pp. 112–13.
52. *ibid.*, p. 115.
53. see James A. Beckford, 'The Embryonic Stage of a Religious Sect's Development: The Jehovah's Witnesses', in ed. Michael Hill, *A Sociological Yearbook of Religion in Britain*, SCM, 1972, and James A. Beckford, *The Trumpet of Prophecy*, Blackwell, 1975.
54. see Bainton, op. cit., p. 157, and Brock, op. cit.
55. *ibid.*, p. 157f.
56. *ibid.*, p. 161.
57. Wilson, op. cit., p. 181, though see Brock, op. cit., p. 20.
58. see Yinger, op. cit., p. 468.

CHAPTER 5

1. Robin Gill, *The Social Context of Theology*, Mowbrays, 1975, chap. 3.
2. *ibid.*, pp. 55–6.
3. E. L. Mascall, *The Secularisation of Christianity*, Libra, 1967, p. 6.
4. *ibid.*, p. 7.
5. Paul van Buren, *The Secular Meaning of the Gospel*, SCM, 1963.
6. John Knox, *The Church and the Reality of Christ*, Collins, 1963.
7. Mascall, op. cit., p. viii.
8. E. L. Mascall, *Up and Down in Adria*, London, 1962.
9. ed. Alec R. Vidler, *Soundings*, Cambridge University Press, 1962.
10. E. L. Mascall, *Theology and Images*, Mowbrays, 1963.
11. A. C. Bridge, *Images of God*, Hodder & Stoughton, 1960.
12. John A. T. Robinson in ed. Robinson and David L. Edwards, *The Honest to God Debate*, SCM, 1963, p. 233.
13. *ibid.*, p. 234.
14. A. M. Ramsey, *Images Old and New*, SPCK, 1963.
15. Alasdair MacIntyre, *Against the Self-Images of the Age*, Duckworth, 1971, p. 25.
16. A. M. Ramsey, *Sacred and Secular*, Longman, 1964.
17. A. M. Ramsey, *God, Christ and the World*, SCM, 1969, pp. 9–10.
18. O. Fielding Clark, *For Christ's Sake*, Religious Education Press, 1963.
19. e.g. J. I. Packer, *Keep Yourselves from Idols*, Church Book Room Press, 1963, Alan Richardson, *Four Anchors from the Stern*, SCM, 1963, Clark, op. cit., and Ramsey, 1963, op. cit.
20. Independent Television, 31 March 1963.
21. *The Sunday Telegraph*, 24 March 1963—see *The Honest to God Debate*, op. cit., p. 95.

22. see *The Honest to God Debate, op. cit.*
23. *ibid.*
24. David L. Edwards in *ibid.*, p. 7.
25. cf. John Poulton, *Dear Archbishop*, Hodder & Stoughton, 1976, p. 149f.
26. see John A. T. Robinson, *But that I can't believe!*, SCM, 1967.
27. John A. T. Robinson, *Honest to God*, SCM, 1963, p. 13.
28. *ibid.*, p. 14.
29. *ibid.*, p. 17.
30. *ibid.*, p. 29.
31. *ibid.*
32. *ibid.*, p. 43.
33. *ibid.*, pp. 45–6.
34. *ibid.*, p. 46.
35. *ibid.*, p. 48.
36. *ibid.*, p. 54.
37. *ibid.*, p. 64.
38. *ibid.*, p. 66.
39. D. M. Baillie, *God Was In Christ*, Faber & Faber, 1956.
40. Robinson, *op. cit.*, p. 73.
41. *ibid.*, pp. 74–5.
42. see John A. T. Robinson, *On Being the Church in the World*, SCM, 1960, and *Liturgy Coming to Life*, SCM, 1963.
43. Robinson, *Honest to God, op. cit.*, p. 85.
44. *ibid.*, pp. 87–8.
45. *ibid.*, p. 91.
46. *ibid.*, p. 97.
47. *ibid.*, p. 99.
48. *ibid.*, p. 105.
49. *ibid.*
50. *ibid.*, p. 106.
51. *ibid.*, pp. 111–12.
52. *ibid.*, p. 114.
53. e.g. D. Rhymes, *No New Morality*, Constable, 1964, cf. Paul Ramsey, *Deeds and Rules in Christian Ethics*, Scottish Journal of Theology Occasional Paper No. 11, 1965. See also, John A. T. Robinson, *Christian Morals Today*, SCM Booklet, 1964.
54. Joseph Fletcher, *Situation Ethics*, SCM, 1966.
55. Robinson, *Honest to God, op. cit.*, p. 123.
56. *ibid.*, p. 124.
57. *ibid.*, p. 123.
58. *ibid.*, p. 124.
59. Alasdair MacIntyre in *The Honest to God Debate, op. cit.*, p. 215.
60. see Robinson in *ibid.*, p. 250.
61. e.g. Alan Richardson, *Religion in Contemporary Debate*, SCM, 1966, and David Jenkins, *Guide to the Debate about God*, SCM, 1966.
62. see Gill, *op. cit.*, chap. 6
63. Mascall, *The Secularisation of Christianity op. cit.*
64. Bryan Wilson, *Religion in Secular Society*, Pelican, 1969, p. 96.
65. see Gill, *op. cit.*, p. 94f.
66. see E. L. Mascall, *Existence and Analogy*, Darton, Longman & Todd, 1949, and John Macquarrie, *God-Talk*, SCM, 1967.
67. Wilson, *op. cit.*, p. 151.

68. cf. Colin Buchanan, *Inflation, Deployment and the Job Prospects of the Clergy*, Grove Books, 1976.
69. cf. Bryan S. Turner, 'The Sociological Explanation of Ecumenicalism', in ed. C. L. Mitton, *The Social Sciences and the Churches*, T. & T. Clark, 1972.
70. see *The Honest to God Debate, op. cit.*, p. 48f.
71. *ibid.*, p. 48.
72. e.g. Mass Observation, *Puzzled People*, 1948.
73. Alasdair MacIntyre in *The Honest to God Debate, op. cit.*, p. 228.
74. David Martin, 'The Secularisation Question', *Theology*, LXXVI, No. 630, Feb. 1973, p. 86.
75. Robinson, *Honest to God, op. cit.*, p. 7.
76. *ibid.*, p. 18.
77. *ibid.*, pp. 26–7.
78. Wilson, *op. cit.*, pp. 97–8.
79. Robinson, *Honest to God, op. cit.*, p. 10.
80. *ibid.*, p. 18.
81. *ibid.*, p. 109.
82. *ibid.*, p. 123.
83. see *The Honest to God Debate, op. cit.*, p. 95f.
84. Robinson, *Honest to God, op. cit.*, p. 41.
85. see Mascall, *op. cit.*
86. John A. T. Robinson, *The New Reformation?*, SCM, 1965, p. 79.
87. John A. T. Robinson, *Exploration into God*, SCM, 1967, p. 14.
88. see Robinson, *But that I can't believe!, op. cit.*
89. see *The Honest to God Debate, op. cit.*
90. cf. Kevin Clements, 'The Religious Variable: Dependent, Independent or Interdependent?' in ed. Michael Hill, *A Sociological Yearbook of Religion in Britain*, SCM, 1971.

CHAPTER 6

1. see Robin Gill, *The Social Context of Theology*, Mowbrays, 1975, chap. 4.
2. Karl Barth, *Evangelical Theology an Introduction*, London, 1963, p. 169.
3. *ibid.*, pp. 169–70. cf. Eduard Thurneysen, *A Theology of Pastoral Care*, John Knox Press, 1962.
4. see F. D. E. Schleiermacher, *Die Praktische Theologie nach den Grundsätzen der Evangelischen Kirche*, Berlin, 1850.
5. Ferdinand Boulard, *An Introduction to Religious Sociology*, Darton, Longman & Todd, 1960, p. 74.
6. see Gill, *op. cit.*, pp. 23–4 and 87–9.
7. Seward Hiltner, *Preface to Pastoral Theology*, New York, 1958, p. 20.
8. cf. Alastair V. Campbell, 'Is Practical Theology Possible?', *Scottish Journal of Theology*, May 1972.
9. Joseph Fletcher, *Situation Ethics*, SCM, 1966, p. 26.
10. *ibid.*, p. 18.
11. *ibid.*, p. 22.
12. see George Wood, 'Situational Ethics', in ed. Ian T. Ramsey, *Christian Ethics and Contemporary Philosophy*, SCM, 1966, essays in ed. Gene H. Outka and Paul Ramsey, *Norm and Context in Christian Ethics*, SCM, 1969.
13. Paul Ramsey, *Deeds and Rules in Christian Ethics*, Scottish Journal of Theology Occasional Papers No, 11, 1965, p. 5.
14. *ibid.*, p. 110. cf. Paul Ramsey, *Nine Modern Moralists*, Prentice-Hall, 1962.

15. see G. R. Dunstan, *The Artifice of Ethics*, SCM, 1974.
16. cf. David Martin, 'Ethical Commentary and Political Decision', *Theology*, Oct. 1973.
17. e.g. Campbell, *op. cit.*
18. J. A. Whyte, 'New Directions in Practical Theology', *Theology*, May 1973, p. 229.
19. Karl Rahner, *Theological Investigations*, Vol. 9, Darton, Longman & Todd, 1972, p. 102.
20. *ibid.*
21. *ibid.*, pp. 104–5.
22. R. W. Hepburn, 'Vision and Choice in Morality', in ed. Ian T. Ramsey, *op. cit.*, p. 181.
23. Paul Lehmann, *Ethics in a Christian Context*, SCM, 1963, p. 14.
24. *ibid.*
25. *ibid.*, p. 45.
26. Paul Ramsey, *op. cit.*, p. 46.
27. David Baily Harned, *Faith and Virtue*, Pilgrim, 1973, p. 14.
28. *ibid.*, p. 9. cf. David Baily Harned, *Grace and Common Life*, University of Virginia, 1971.
29. Stanley Hauerwas, *Character and the Christian Life*, Trinity University, 1975, p. 3.
30. Stanley Hauerwas, *Vision and Virtue*, Fides, 1974, p. 2. cf. Keith Ward, *The Divine Image*, SPCK, 1976.
31. see ed. James F. Childress and David Baily Harned, *Secularisation and the Protestant Prospect*, Westminster, 1970.
32. see Gill, *op. cit.*
33. cf. Martin, *op. cit.*
34. see John A. T. Robinson, *Christian Morals Today*, SCM Booklet, 1964.
35. Talcott Parsons, *The Social System*, Routledge & Kegan Paul, 1951, p. 367.
36. Gregory Baum, *Religion and Alienation*, Paulist, 1975, p. 1.
37. e.g. Rosemary Ruether, *Faith and Fratricide*, Seabury, 1974, cf. Gregory Baum, *The Jews and the Gospel*, Bloomsbury, 1961 and Charlotte Klein, 'Vatican View of Jewry, 1939–62', *Christian Attitudes on Jews and Judaism*, No. 43, Aug. 1975, and 'The Vatican and German-Italian Antisemitism in the Nineteen-Thirties', *Judacia*, Sept. 1975.
38. Baum, *Religion and Alienation, op. cit.*, p. 76.
39. *ibid.*, p. 77.
40. see Charles Y. Glock and Rodney Stark, *Christian Beliefs and Anti-Semitism*, Harper, 1966, Richard L. Gorsuch and Daniel Aleshire, 'Christian Faith and Prejudice: Review of Research', *Journal for the Scientific Study of Religion*, Vol. 13, No. 3, 1974.
41. Baum. *op. cit.*, p. 10.
42. *ibid.*, p. 83. cf. Francis Schüssler Fiorenza, 'Critical Social Theory and Christology', in *Proceedings of the 30th Annual Convention of the Catholic Theological Society of America*, New Orleans, 1975.
43. see essays in Ian T. Ramsey, *op. cit.*, and James M. Gustafson, *Can Ethics be Christian?*, University of Chicago, 1975.
44. see Alasdair MacIntyre, *A Short History of Ethics*, Routledge & Kegan Paul, 1967, Maria Ossowska, *Social Determinants of Moral Ideas*, Routledge & Kegan Paul, 1971, and John H. Barnsley, *The Social Reality of Ethics*, Routledge & Kegan Paul, 1972.

45. Charles E. Raven, *The Theological Basis of Christian Pacifism*, The Fellow-ship of Reconciliation, 1952, p. 1.
46. *ibid.*, p. 37f.
47. Paul Ramsey, *op. cit.*, p. 110.
48. see Raven, *op. cit.*
49. cf. G. H. C. Macgregor, *The New Testament Basis of Pacifism*, James Clarke, 1936.
50. see F. W. Dillistone, *Charles Raven: Naturalist, Historian and Theologian*, Hodder & Stoughton, 1975: John H. Yoder, *Karl Barth and the Problem of War*, Abingdon, 1970.
51. Raven, *op. cit.*, p. 22.
52. see Bryan Wilson, *Magic and the Millenium*, Heinemann, 1973, p. 18f.
53. cf. Eberhard Welty, *A Handbook of Christian Social Ethics*, Nelson, 1963, Vol. 2.
54. cf. T. R. Milford, *The Valley of Decision: the Christian Dilemma in the Nuclear Age*, British Council of Churches, 1961.
55. see J. Milton Yinger, *The Scientific Study of Religion*, Collier-Macmillan, 1970, p. 467f.
56. see Dillistone, *op. cit.*
57. cf. United Reformed Church, *Non-Violent Action*, SCM, 1973.
58. see Peter Brock, *Pacifism in Europe to 1914*, Princeton University Press, and Peter Brock, *Twentieth-Century Pacifism*, Van Nostrand Reinhold, 1970.
59. cf. Yinger, *op. cit.*, and Bryan Wilson, *Religious Sects*, Weidenfeld & Nicolson, 1970, p. 181.
60. e.g. Milford, *op. cit.*
61. e.g. Welty, *op. cit.*
62. see Paul Ramsey, *op. cit.*, and Hauerwas, *Character and the Christian Life*, *op. cit.*
63. see Parsons, *op. cit.*, p. 379.

CHAPTER 7

1. cf. Karl Mannheim, *Ideology and Utopia*, Routledge & Kegan Paul, 1936, p. 40f, and Peter Hamilton, *Knowledge and Social Structure*, Routledge & Kegan Paul, 1974.
2. Max Weber, *The Protestant Ethic and the 'Spirit' of Capitalism*, Scribner, 1958.
3. *ibid.*, p. 35.
4. see Gerhard E. Lenski, *The Religious Factor*, Doubleday, 1961, and ed. Charles Y. Glock & Phillip E. Hammond, *Beyond the Classics?*, *Essays in the Scientific Study of Religion*, Harper & Row, 1973, pp. 113–30.
5. see Gary D. Bouma, 'Recent "Protestant Ethic" Research', *Journal for the Scientific Study of Religion*, Vol. 21, No. 2, 1973.
6. Gregory Baum, *Religion and Alienation*, Paulist Press, 1975, p. 85.
7. *ibid.*, p. 164.
8. see Alistair Kee, *A Reader in Political Theology*, SCM, 1974.
9. cf. Robert N. Bellah, *Beyond Belief*, Harper & Row, 1970, p. 240.
10. see Robin Gill, *The Social Context of Theology*, Mowbrays, 1975, p. 12.
11. Roderick Martin, 'Sociology and Theology' in ed. D. E. H. Whiteley and R. Martin, *Sociology, Theology and Conflict*, Blackwell, 1969, p. 36.

Author Index

148

Subject Index

Micro-sociology 17–18, 23, 75
Militarism 38, 71–81, 124–8
Mission 64
Mixed Agapism 110
Monotheism 18, 33–4
Morality (see also Christian Ethics) 89, 93–4, 96, 101
Moral Philosophy 115, 122
Mormons 46–7

Naturalism 91
Neo-liberalism 33
Neo-orthodoxy 4, 83
Neutrality 65
Non-violent Action 126
Norms xiii, 4, 109, 126

Ordinands 106
Ordination of women 75
Original Sin 126
Origins of Theology 8–9, 12, 23, 29, 34, 129
Orthopraxis 119

Pacifism 36–43, 58, 71–81, 123–8
Parousia 78–9, 125
Particular Ideology 10
Pax Romana 39, 41
Pelagianism 126
Pharisees 121
Phenomenology 1
Plausibility Structures 85, 118
Pluralism xiii, 33, 35
Political Determinants 5, 19, 33–5, 41, 48, 57–8, 79
Political Ideology 5
Political Theology 83
Popular Theology 68, 89, 99, 103
Positivists 9, 11, 15
Practical Theology xiii, 4, 105–28
Pragmatism 126
Prayer 89, 92–3
Pre-literate Religion 3
Prescriptive Christian Ethics xiii, 106, 109–11
Prescriptive Practical Theology xiii, 106–9
Process Theology 83–4
Proclamation 106–7
Protestant-Ethic Thesis 18–19, 65–70, 130–4
Protestantism 28, 46, 63

Quaker House 80
Quakers 37, 77–80, 126
Quantitative Correlations 13–14, 24

Racism 65
Reductionism xi, 7–8
Reformation 63, 67, 102, 115
Relationism 13
Relativism xi, 11–13, 29, 64
Religious Affiliation 47, 69
Religious Belief 2–5, 119–20
Religious Emotion 3
Religious Enclaves 35
Religious Experience 3
Religious Practice 47, 121
Religious Sociology 107–8
Respect for Persons 127
Response to the World 42
Reverence for Life 127
Roman Catholicism—see Catholicism
Roman Empire 14, 30–1, 33, 41, 56–9

Science 15
Sectarianism 32, 35, 48, 58, 125, 128
Sects 35–7, 42, 77–80, 125–8
Secularisation 20, 32–3, 35, 61–2, 85, 96, 98, 117
Secular Theology 61, 84, 96
Sequelae of Beliefs 2–3, 30, 36, 84, 119, 123
Sermon on the Mount 38
Shepherding 108
Situation Ethics 94, 96, 109–11, 122
Social Change 15, 28, 112
Social Consequences xiii, 118–22
Social Context ix–xi, 11, 30–1, 85, 107, 118, 121
Social Determinants x–xii, 12, 15, 17–18, 21–3, 27–59, 61, 72–3, 85, 123, 127, 129–30, 132–4
Socialisation 23, 129
Social Significance xi–xii, 15, 18, 21–3, 28–9, 58–9, 61–103, 123, 129–30, 133–4
Social Variables xiii, 45, 105–28
Socio-cultural Determinants 31–3, 40–1, 45, 56–7
Socio-ecclesiastical Determinants 35–6, 40–2, 45, 58
Sociology of Ethics 123
Sociology of Ideology 1

152